Writing for Performance

TEACHING WRITING

Volume 5

Series Editor

Patricia Leavy
USA

Scope

The *Teaching Writing* series publishes concise instructional writing guides. Series books each focus on a different subject area, discipline or type of writing. The books are intended to be used in undergraduate and graduate courses across the disciplines and can also be read by individual researchers or students engaged in thesis work.

Series authors must have a demonstrated publishing record and must hold a PhD, MFA or the equivalent. Please email queries to the series editor at pleavy7@aol.com

Writing for Performance

Anne Harris and Stacy Holman Jones
Monash University, Australia

SENSE PUBLISHERS
ROTTERDAM/BOSTON/TAIPEI

A C.I.P. record for this book is available from the Library of Congress.

ISBN: 978-94-6300-592-0 (paperback)
ISBN: 978-94-6300-593-7 (hardback)
ISBN: 978-94-6300-594-4 (e-book)

Published by: Sense Publishers,
P.O. Box 21858,
3001 AW Rotterdam,
The Netherlands
https://www.sensepublishers.com/

All chapters in this book have undergone peer review.

Printed on acid-free paper

PRAISE FOR
WRTING FOR PERFORMANCE

"What a welcome, insightful and much-needed book *Writing for Performance* is. Authors Anne Harris and Stacy Holman Jones bring us to an integrated notion of writing that is embodied, felt, breathed and flung from stage to page and back again. This important book is thrilling in both its theorizing and its usefulness as it sets out potential roadmaps of how we can conjure writing daring to explore the heat and sparks of race, class, sex and gender. *Writing for Performance* will become a crucial text for the creation of the performance and theater that the 21st Century will need."
– Tim Miller, artist and author of *Body Blows: Six Performances* and *1001 Beds: Performances, Essays and Travels*

"No prescriptions here. Instead, a thoughtful and pedagogical rumination on the ideas of writing and performance, ideas which often materialize into pleasing products, to be sure, but whose wondrous processes can remain clandestine. In the hands of this creative duo, however, we find a deep and abiding respect for the many creative processes that might fuel writing and performance that matters. From the deep wells of their own experiences, Harris and Holman Jones offer exercises that are not meant to mold the would-be writer, but spur them on to recognize their latent writing/ performative selves."
– Kathleen Gallagher, Distinguished Professor of Curriculum, Teaching, and Learning, University of Toronto

"*Writing for Performance* embodies the practicality of craft and possibilities for transcendence necessary in any writing and performance pedagogy. Replete with clear description and example, Harris and Holman Jones invite the reader/practitioner/performer/scholar into their own abilities to engage word and body for the purpose of meaning making and personal/political transformation."
– Tami Spry, Professor of Performance Studies, St. Cloud State University

"*Writing for Performance* is a much-needed text that synthetically weaves the dynamics of words, bodies, spaces and things in the integrative process of writing in/as performance and performance in/as writing. The authors engage systematically inflected and reflected forms of experience as the source materials (or equipment) in building grammatical aesthetic expressions in theatre and performance studies. It is the textbook that I wanted when I was struggling to find my own writerly voice in the shifting modes of the personal and professional, and in the presumed tensions between the performative and academic zones of my intersectional identities."
– Bryant Keith Alexander, Professor of Communication, Performance, Cultural and Pedagogical Studies and Dean of the College of Communication and Fine Arts, Loyola Marymount University

"What's exciting about this book: the bridges it builds between imagining, devising, writing, performing—many bridges for many different purposes. In *Writing for Performance,* Anne Harris and Stacy Holman Jones, as experienced theatre-makers, practitioners and scholars, provide a personalized blueprint for writing—no easy, one-size-fits-all answers—but instead a rich array of models of practice in which the voice of the writer, in the process of creating the theatre event, can be heard clearly, honestly and provocatively. And, the most important message coming through the exemplars, the theoretical considerations and the exercises for writing: put the words on the page."
– Christine Sinclair, Melbourne Graduate School of Education and Head of Drama Education, The University of Melbourne

"Anne Harris and Stacy Holman Jones bring their rich and varied theatrical experiences into this intriguing, behind-the-scenes look at how performance is not just written but revised and devised for formal presentation. The co-authors include evocative texts and scripts that demonstrate the multiple styles of dramatic narrative, along with a series of practical exercises to extend the writer's creative capacities. Harris and Holman Jones offer perceptive and nurturing guidance for the development of performative work by artists, poets, researchers, and community-based fieldworkers."
– Johnny Saldaña, Evelyn Smith Professor of Theatre, Arizona State University

"*Writing for Performance* presents a helpful overview of ways writers—as individuals or members of a company—generate performances. The authors place these methods and approaches in historical perspective, highlighting strategies beyond the "well-made play," but without underestimating its influence. They also provide a diverse set of concrete exemplars and exercises that readers can work through alone or as part of a classroom or other creative community. I particularly appreciated their overall perspective, which situates such writing as a fundamentally aesthetic, ethical, and pedagogical act that goes beyond the construction of literary artifacts to consider how discussion, devising, and eventual performance and documentation play a crucial role in the construction, sharing, and critique of social knowledge. That Harris and Holman Jones accomplish all of this in such a warm, accessible, and ultimately encouraging way helps to demystify the writing process, providing support for both the novice coming to performance for the first time and the experienced writer who may want to branch out and try new ways of working in academic, professional, and community performance situations."
– Craig Gingrich-Philbrook, Professor of Performance Studies, Southern Illinois University

"The mystique of the writer in the writing process often discourages engagement. What and Anne Harris and Stacy Holman Jones have achieved here demystifies the sometimes clouded and makes clear the often hidden in writing and performance (and the relationship between them). That they manage to do this in an artful and poetic way is a testament to their agility as thinkers, performers and writers. This clear, insightful and occasionally provocative work will be indispensable for those who hope to create compelling writing and performance."
– Michael Anderson, Professor of Education, The University of Sydney

I dedicate my work in this book to Maria Irene Fornes and Morgan Jenness, two fierce and talented women of the New York theatre who have inspired and taught me on many fronts, only one of which is writing for performance.

Fornes is one of the greatest American playwrights of all time and was an inspiring teacher to me in the 1980s at New York University (NYU). She is currently 85 years old and lives in a nursing home in New York City, largely thanks to Jenness, who brought her back to the city to be near friends and those who can look after her, and who loves and memorialises her frequently and unconditionally, online and in person. What I most remember of Fornes at NYU: her advice was, "write well, break the rules, say something that matters."

Morgan Jenness is a legendary dramaturg, literary agent, activist and theatre history teacher whom I met when I was 17 years old, through her legendary work with Joseph Papp at The New York Public Theatre, and through the Young Playwrights Festival which she helped establish.

Both women have made immeasurable contributions to writing for the theatre, and should be much more widely recognised for their contributions. I thank you both for your brilliance, and for your lives of artful service—gracias amigas!
– Anne

I dedicate my work and words to all of the 'students' I've worked with in writing and performance over the years, who of course have become my teachers, too: Adrian Amor, A.B., Adolfo Lagomasino, Nicole Embree, Christopher McRae, Summer Cunningham, Sarah Dykins Callahan, Elizabeth Edgecomb, David Purnell, Linda Levitt, Patrick Santoro, and Wendy Adams. The list goes on.
– Stacy

TABLE OF CONTENTS

ACKNOWLEDGEMENTS

We would like to thank the following individuals and collectives for their inspiration, input, and contributions to this book: Patricia Leavy for the great book series and the opportunity to be a part of it; Prue Wales and the IDEIRI community; Sean Tobin at Singapore School of the Arts/Singapore Fringe Festival; Christine Sinclair; Rachel Forgasz; Tim Miller; Joel Radcliffe, Roz Ward, all at Safe Schools Coalition; Tiffany Jones and Emily Gray; Amy Kilgard, A.B., Adrian Amor, Carrie Rudzinski, Ryan Haddad, Rachel McKibbens, members of the California State University, Northridge Performance Ensemble, and Rena Petrello.

It's not always easy to love your collaborators, nor to collaborate with lovers. Anne is feeling pretty damn lucky to have found both in Stacy Holman Jones. And for all our other shared affective performances that lead into and away from this text, I thank you more than you can know.

Stacy is feeling pretty damn lucky, too, to have found in Anne a lover, collaborator, and someone to see all kinds of performance with—even the kinds that teenage daughters would pronounce 'annoying', 'weird' or just plain 'pointless'. After the words "I love you", whether it's the first or the 500th time you've heard them, there's nothing sweeter than hearing the words "I love your writing," especially when you're trying to finish a book. Anne, I love you and your writing too.

Lastly, to Haddie, Murphy, and Tasha: you fill our days with hugs/pets, crooked/beautiful smiles, and reasons to get up from the writing table and out into the world. And to dear old loony Luna (1998–2015): you are missed immeasurably in this domestic community of performers and writers. We still smell your baby smell.

EXEMPLARS

WRITING EXERCISES

BEGINNINGS

WHAT IS WRITING FOR PERFORMANCE?

When we first discussed the need for a book of this kind, we thought of it as 'writing plays, scripts, and performance texts.' But writing for performance is much more than this. A text that is written for or with the express purpose of performance can be a play, a series of monologues, or a performance blueprint or map, but it can be many other things as well. Sometimes writers do not know they are going to need or want a written textual document of the performance work they have created. Sometimes performance texts come into being for the purpose of publication, dissemination, or teaching. Ultimately, performance texts can take as many shapes, sizes, forms, and structures as there are reasons for their existence.

Writing and performance are too often contrasted as different and at times contradictory practices: performance is 'embodied', while writing is 'a record' of the 'event', especially within academic contexts. This book rejects that view, and asserts instead that writing and performance are two arms on the same body. If performance-making is a practice of inscription, writing is equally a physical practice. It is a making practice, a creative practice, a critical practice; these are not particularly contentious aspects of creative writing, especially writing for performance. But writing as a physical act continues to fire debates about embodiment, virtuality, criticality, affect, and abstraction.

Writers use space strategically, if often opportunistically, writing in public and alternatively in private, but always physical places. Most writers (both academic and non-academic) talk specifically about the spaces they need in which to make their work (like any other maker), and in which to see their work performed. Writers have different practices and proclivities about their sonic and aural surroundings as well as their physical ones, and ways of improving or ameliorating range from absolute silence to programming one's environment. Writers have environmental requirements, biases, even fetishes and obsessions: some writers can only write with music playing, others cannot write if there is any noise at all in their environment.

Avoiding or immersing oneself in company, even writing in the middle of the night (to optimise silence) are just a few temporal, spatial, and aural tricks we use. We have found that during intense periods of everyday writing (as when we are under deadline and write 10–12 hours per day), our bodies become increasingly rebellious—hurting, aching, cramping, and gaining weight. We play tricks on our bodies to persuade them to allow us to write for as many repetitive hours as we like or need.

Yet it's a balancing act: as much as writing is an embodied and spatial practice, it's also a temporal practice, one takes place not only in space but also in time. Once we slip 'out' of the writing process, the breach can be for a few moments or sometimes for months on end. The 'flow' (Csikszentmihalyi) remains a magical state, one that transcends both time and place, and when we are in it, time evaporates largely unnoticed. And when we are not (cue crickets SFX), time stands still. Many writers have favourite writing tools: particular kinds of pens, typewriters, or word processing fonts, which help us write through time and—as we write *about* time—that help us travel into our memories.

Amidst all of this, writing is an act of performance.

It often begins as a private performance—or sometimes a collaborative performance between co-writers—but always ends in a kind of performance for others, whether in a page-based performance for readers, or a stage- or other-public performances in/by/with moved bodies or even—increasingly—in virtual and extended performances that include human, posthuman, and more-than-human bodies.

Just as performance texts can be *encountered* in different ways, performance texts can be *generated* in different ways (either by beginning in diverse and divergent ways or by featuring different elements/experiences). This book introduces readers to some ways to both encounter and to generate a range of performance texts.

For example, Stacy's training in performance studies informs our discussions of devising performance, site-specific performance, and narrative, poetic performance. For Stacy, audiencing and creating performance works often originate in felt experiences and move toward scripted stages and/or texts. Her training focuses on the relationship between live and improvisational performance and scripting, led by 'on the floor' processes. Anne's training in playwriting/screenwriting and her work as a professional playwright informs our sections on playwriting, screenwriting, lesbian and queer theatre, writing one-person shows, performance poetry and feminist theatre. Her work is based in page-to-stage theatrical works that start with words and progress through scripting, dramaturgy, directing, design, and ultimately into (mostly) collaborative production experiences. We don't use these differences to imply a binary difference that is linear (either script-to-performance, or performance-to-script), but rather to recognise that writing specifically for and with performance can take many shapes and directions, sometimes multiple directions at once. Throughout this text, we track examples from our work and incorporate short examples from a more expansive list of works from other performance makers and writers as well.

We also acknowledge in this brief introduction that there are global trends and intersecting flows that affect the diverse forms, contexts, and practices of writing for performance. For example, any global overview of the various forms of performance texts (plays, performance art, solo performance, etc.) must address the question of audience: what does the particular performance text type aim to say, what 'work' does it aim to do, or goals does it have? What individual elements does that work necessarily demand? What particular and unique features, characteristics, and voices do those text types deploy?

Lastly, while attending to the particulars of writing various kinds of performance texts, we've written this book—another type of performance text—around the principle that despite their unique characteristics and idiosyncrasies, performance texts share the four common characteristics of: words, embodiments, spaces, and things. These interrelating components of writing for performance weave themselves into and through one another, allowing us to address these themes in relation to one another (words as embodiments, spaces as texts, things as embodiments, etc.). That is why, after years of performing, writing, and reading texts about performance and how to write performatively, we have chosen to create a synthetic guide to writing for performance, rather than approach the task by focusing on an over-simplified treatment of genres or by offering a practical guide that does not address the relationship between the work, the audience, and its context. Here, we use words, bodies, spaces, and things as our four pivots for understanding how writing for performance must be conducted in relation to other people, places, objects, histories, and practices. In the final two chapters in the book, we take up rehearsing and performing in the context of a specific performance text. While it is not within the scope of this book to cover the processes of rehearsing and performing in their entirety, they are stages of development in writing for performance that have an enormous impact on the living word that forms its blueprint.

By organising the book in this way, we invite you to see the relationships among each component of performance: how can you write for performance without words, without bodies, outside of time and space, without things and symbolic tools? Similarly, we suggest, it is impossible to construct performance texts without bodies. These bodies take up embodiments—they realize or express something in a tangible form—of many kinds, including bodies in rehearsal, bodies in devising collaborations, and bodies on stage. Yet embodiments are not limited to human bodies; indeed, a book like this is itself an embodiment of performance writing, another 'body' and space that holds the symbols and words of a performance, one that has happened or is going to happen in the future. The notion of embodiment itself is called into question here with a discussion of virtual embodiment and a consideration of the ways in which virtual embodiments are increasingly performed as part of everyday online/offline worlds, and in conjunction with 'offline' bodies-in-spaces in productive and proliferating ways. We offer the following history of writing for performance to situate our own consideration of words, things, and bodies of many kinds in both time and space.

THE WORK OF THE (WESTERN) WORD

While we acknowledge the long and diverse histories of non-Western performance and their accompanying textual traditions, this book will focus primarily on Western performance traditions and types as the traditions from which we have emerged and in which we have been trained.

Aristotelian Dramatic Structure

Although Romans were the first to divide dramatic performances into sections (or acts), the Greeks are credited with the birth of Western theatre. More specifically, between approximately 500–400 BC, the 'fabulous four' (Sophocles, Euripides, Aristophanes and Eschylus) are credited with the birth of roughly our contemporary Western approach to what has come to be known as 'comedy' and 'tragedy', although these categories meant very different things to the Greeks than they do to contemporary audiences. In addition to these four theorists, about 100 years later the Greek dramatist Aristotle's (384–322 BC) plays and his major analytic work *The Poetics* (written in 350 BC) contributed what is usually considered the remainder of the conceptual foundations and creative basis of Western theatre (particularly tragedy). It was called *The Poetics* because drama in Greek and Roman times was still written in—and considered—a form of performed poetry. What remains of *The Poetics* offers the first dramatic theoretical outline of 'good principles' for theatrical work. His analysis of theatre (tragedy) as a literary and performative genre includes characteristics that were particularly apparent in *Oedipus*, a play by Sophocles that Aristotle considered the perfect example of tragedy. Aristotelean drama is an imitation of an action (*mimesis*) not narrative, must provide audiences an opportunity for catharsis, and is formally proscriptive and not concerned with character or with content per se. Aristotelean dramas must be 'whole', containing a discernable beginning, middle and end; aim for a unity of time, place and action; and must include the six defining parts: plot, character, diction, thought, song, and spectacle.

The 'Well-Made Play' (19th Century-Modern Times)

The 'well-made play' is a 19th-century term that describes the pervasive approach to theatrical scriptwriting in commercial or mainstream theatre that prioritises suspense, formulaic plot, and neat resolution of the central complication in three acts. It is usually structured to include the following five stages: exposition (and introduction of major dramatic question), complication/inciting incident, climax/crisis/turning point, resolution, and *denouement*. Other theatre analysts characterise the well-made play by its components rather than plot stages. Well-made plays are always in part judged against their success in achieving neatness, complexity, and theatrical effectiveness in executing their predetermined problem and pattern. By the early 20th century, playwriting instruction and their manuals had formalized the well-made play as the primary approach to writing for theatre.

The well-made play centres upon a tightly controlled plot, subplots (or complications) that relate to the central tension or question of the play, and the resolution of the plot which always ends in fulfillment of the 'hero's journey' (in which case, in Aristotelian terms, the play can be characterised as a comedy) or the failure of the hero to resolve her/his challenge (which makes it, in Aristotelian terms, a tragedy). The requisite *denouement* (French for 'untying') is sometimes referred to as the 'falling action', where the loose ends resulting from the climax are cleared up.

While it is often derogatorily regarded as old-fashioned and uninventive, this format still dominates much playwriting instruction, musical and mainstream theatre, and typical Hollywood film formats. Well-known 20th-century playwrights who employed this format in whole or part include George Bernard Shaw, Henrik Ibsen, Anton Chekhov, and Oscar Wilde.

Modern Playwriting (20th Century)

It is impossible to talk about a singular 'modern' playwriting or theatre-making style, process, or approach. Books and courses love to typify styles and approaches according to a linear characterisation, but these books—written in the Western world—typically only draw on Western drama, and this usually means American and British. Of course, theatre goes far beyond such constraints, and in many ways the most innovative work often emerges from less dominant paradigms and contexts. August Strindberg is one European example, a Swedish playwright (and compulsive writer in many other forms) who was extremely experimental for his time, although he may seem to the contemporary reader or actor more traditional than he did then. However, his experiments with surrealism, symbolism, and character have influenced subsequent generations of playwrights worldwide. Indeed, there have been many innovations to the 'well-made play' over the past 150 years, and many involve a turn toward devised, physical, or agit prop (agitation-propoganda, i.e., political) theatre rather than text-based theatre.

Feminist/Non-Naturalistic/Ensemble Theatre (1960s-Present)

Feminist, non-naturalistic, and ensemble theatre work takes a collaborative and collective ensemble-based approach to making theatre. One leader of feminist theatre is Maria Irene Fornes is a Cuban-American playwright who was a leading figure of the New York avant garde theatre scene in the 1960s and 1970s (she also worked as a designer, costumier, writer, actor and director). A dedicated teacher (Anne took classes with her at New York University's Dramatic Writing program), Fornes paved the way for Latina/Latino voices on American and world stages and influenced a generation of playwrights concerned with poverty, gender, and class politics. Her play *Fefu and Her Friends* (1977), among others, showed young playwrights of the time that theatre did not have to conform to particular structures or subject matter.

Caryl Churchill is frequently considered the 'mother' of non-traditional theatre, has been called the 'David Bowie' of experimental theatre, and the theatre maker who has brought home the links between formal innovations with political content. She is not alone in changing the relationship between modern playwrights to their writing, but her impact on playscript forms and formats cannot be underestimated. Drawing on a range of influences, including Antonin Artaud's Theater of Cruelty (which encouraged theatre that assaulted the senses of audiences in efforts to tap into the subconscious emotions and fears of the audience), Churchill has always been concerned with abuses of power, both domestic and public. She expertly weaves the personal and political together in ways that few other playwrights have done, and while her work is famously considered 'feminist', it is more universally concerned with the ways in which abuses in the domestic sphere affect and are affected by the public sphere—not only amongst/for women. Her most recent work addresses the conflict in Palestine/Israel. Churchill's approach importantly included a company working with her as playwright, an approach which combines the generative richness of group devising with the ability to hone and lock that becomes possible in playscripting. Ensemble work, whether as an acting company or for devising/writing work, is challenging and often includes time and space demands that many theatre makers simply do not have today. However, those like Churchill, who are able to both write adaptations and original plays and then devise the production within ensembles, create works that are robust and complexly layered. Ensemble devising that works with/results in a playscript can take advantage of the best of both approaches (fine-tuned writing and on-the-floor, embodied processes), and there are many robust examples of current theatre makers (like PearlDamour company, profiled in Chapter 5, for example) who are employing and extending these approaches.

Another example is Anne Bogart's and Tadashi Suzuki's SITI Company, which trains practitioners in the Viewpoints approach (primarily based in acting), and which results in theatre pieces that are not text-driven. As the SITI website highlights, "The Viewpoints and the Suzuki Method are two distinct methods of actor training used in building and staging SITI productions" and while these are acting skills the works that result are immediately recognisable. One example of their recent work is the show 'Steel Hammer' (http://siti.org/content/production/steel-hammer), which grew out of an oratorio written by composer Julia Wolfe and devised performance work by the SITI Company. A complex example of this kind of performance-making, their website describes its links to the historical figure of John Henry and "the ever-widening circles of resonance that ripple out from this American story of the 1870s." Specific points of thematic interest include:

- Work and the cost of hard labor on the human body and soul.
- The human impulse to tell a story.
- The necessity for stories in our lives.
- The function of stories in society.
- How stories travel through time.

- Who owns a story?
- The thrill of a story.

Growing out of the already-existent music by Wolfe, the SITI Company actors worked to develop their own movement and embodiment before combining to collaborate for a workshop production at Louisville's Humana Festival in 2014. For text, Anne Bogart invited four playwrights (Kia Corthron, Will Power, Carl Hancock Rux, and Regina Taylor) to write "10-minute versions of the John Henry story in a way that felt true to them." The original texts that they developed based on this classic tale became a fourth component interwoven with embodiment, space, and sound, a component approach that we have used in our approach to this book.

Live Art, Happenings, and Solo Performance (1960s-Present)

'Experimental' or non-traditional forms of theatre can be scripted or unscripted, improvisational or rehearsed, solo or collective. The kind of spontaneous public performance known as 'happenings' originated and were most popular in the 1950s–1960s (but are again on the rise especially including new media) and involved public venues, audience participation, and multiple artforms (dance, music, solo performance, etc.). Happenings were designed to involve the audience in the creation of th work, focusing attention on the ephemeral or fleeting nature of 'live' performance and asking critical questions about the nature of 'art'. One recent example of 'happenings' are the 'flashmob' phenomenon, in which a group of people break into seemingly-spontaneous dance, song, or other performance, in public spaces.

From the 1990s forward, performance makers like Spalding Gray, Tim Miller, Anna Deavere Smith, and Lisa Kron have advanced the form into complex and often less agit prop performance styles. Smith, like our exemplar in Chapters 6 and 7 (*Out/In Front: Teaching Change* and *Heavier Than Air*), uses conversations with real life people (documentary theatre to some) to script performances centered around a community, an issue, or happening and a political theme. Solo performers also often work with a large (and sometimes ongoing) collective or team of collaborators to devise shows that are performed only largely alone. Precursors to solo performance include vaudeville and before that the tradition of troubadours; contemporary extensions of solo performance include performance and slam poetry.

Canon and context (both historical as theatre/performance history, and literary) are crucial to understanding where each writer's contribution to performance writing sits, but there are larger sociocultural considerations as well, and these considerations impact both what ends up *in* the performance and how the performance is received.

ASKING AESTHETIC, CRITICAL, AND ETHICAL QUESTIONS

What is the relationship of the individual's story and social commentary present in the text? How does social commentary/critique and get realized in performance work, and how might this commentary change from 'stage to the page'? What does it mean to write something that is created in order to be performed? Is the performance *text*, then, a full realisation of the performance, or a plan or blueprint which gestures toward (without realizing) the embodied life of the performance?

We are not the first to ask such aesthetic, critical, and ethical questions in relation to practical 'making' considerations in performance writing. Yet in order to ask these kinds of questions, we recognise that there are inherent political projects and commitments embedded in performance writing, and we ask how these political projects are created and/or realized in aesthetically different texts for performance? These questions suggest both historical and also aesthetic considerations. For example, how can the recent commercial success and formal innovation of Lisa Kron and Jeanine Tesori's Broadway musical *Fun Home* (adapted from Alison Bechdel's graphic novel of the same name and touted as the first mainstream musical about a young lesbian; see Thomas) be understood in relation to Tony Kuschner's *Angels in America,* an exampimation of AIDS in America, generation ago? How can performance makers who 'write' their scripts as a secondary (not primary) act of creation/development be understood alongside playwrights who begin with the word (looking, for example, at Anna Deavere Smith's *Twilight: Los Angeles* about the 1992 Los Angeles Riots and Moises Kaufman's and Tectonic Theatre Project's *The Laramie Project*, about the murder of Matthew Shepard)? How can non-naturalistic approaches to play-making be compared across wide cultural and formal differences, such as those used by British feminist political maker Caryl Churchill, Cuban playwright Maria Irene Fornes, and Anne Bogart's work in her collaborations with the SITI company? Or how to view playwrights like Suzan Lori Parks' commentary on African American experience (in, for example, *Topdog/Underdog*) next to Kuschner's writing of political and gay male histories as both 'text-based playwrights' when they create such wildly different kinds of social critique in their work?

Further, what are the roles and productive tensions of these considerations when working with performance ensembles—especially student ensembles—when it is inevitable that students will write 'bad' (sometimes offensive, sometimes stereotyping, often objectifying) social commentary texts, at least initially? Can polemical performance making and playscripting be useful either aesthetically or socially? How can directors, devisers, teachers, and collaborators encourage others to think about an ethics of representation regarding the portrayal of 'others' onstage, and what right, responsibility, or prohibition does every performance maker have to do so? There are as many forms of theatre 'with a message' as there are formal approaches and innovations. Think, for example, of the many names and styles of research-informed theatre (Belliveau & Lea, 2016), including (but not limited to): verbatim theatre (David Hare, Moises Kaufman, Anna Deavere-Smith, *My Name is Rachel Corrie* by Alan Rickman and Katharine Viner); performance autoethnography (Dwight Conquergood, Soyini Madison, E. Patrick Johnson, Tami Spry), applied theatre (Peter O'Connor & Michael Anderson) and other versions of adapting research or factual data into fictionalised performance works (see, for example the Australian theatre-in-education play *Blackrock* by Nick Enright, and our discussion of queer teachers transcripts-to-performance in Chapters 6 and 7). Above all, questions about the intersections of aesethtics, critique, and ethics, along with the diverse approaches to writing and making performance detailed above, should inform and serve your writing work, not limit it. In this book, we hope to help you put language and skills to some of these forms and questions, not be constrained by them.

WHO IS THIS BOOK FOR?

No one text can do everything, and the aim of this brief book is particularly specific: to offer a practical and concise introductory guide to those wishing to write performance texts in a range of forms, contexts, and approaches. As an introductory text, it cannot cover in depth the great range of ways that writers research, write, revise, and stage diverse performance texts. However, it can and does provide a historical and contemporary overview of performance writing and some ways to approach the doing of it. While those who identify as solo performance artists may approach the writing of their performance texts very differently than a young writer who is completing a Masters of Fine Arts in playwriting, this text hopes to offer both writers some basics of form and new ideas for approaching and understanding the core steps in that work.

This book speaks to undergraduate and post-graduate students of playwriting; theatre and performance studies; and ethnographic, arts-based, collaborative and community performance makers who wish to learn the how-to of writing for performance. Other qualitative researchers too will use this book to learn the basics of researching, devising, writing, revising, and mounting a range of performance texts, including those drawing on qualitative and in some cases quantitative data as the basis for your performance text. While attempting to cover a wide range of performance writing forms, we do so through an holistically-structured approach, stepping readers through the stages of writing plays and other scripts, as well as auto/ethnographic, collaborative, ensemble, community-based, spoken word, multimedia/hybrid, and experimental approaches to that work. Teachers and facilitators can use each chapter to take their students through the conceptualizing, writing process, and performing/creating process, supported by exemplars that illustrate the writing strategies at work in each chapter. Taken together, this text offers both academic and non-academic audiences a comprehensive guide for creating dynamic texts for performance.

ABOUT THIS BOOK AND ITS STRUCTURE

Each chapter includes several exemplars that illustrate the discussion focus of each chapter, followed by "how to" exercises and/or writing prompts so readers can try the form themselves. In a practical move, we have chosen to structure the book around the 'tools' of performance writing—words, bodies, things, and spaces, while acknowledging the overlap of these elements in all genres of performance writing. The final two chapters, Rehearsing/Devising and Revising/Performing, profile a single example—the development of an original interview-based play—to show how much even a fully scripted performance text changes during the period of rehearsal and production. We conclude by encouraging readers to try exercising their creative muscles in all of these forms, knowing that mastery makes way for creative innovation. Below we offer a quick summary of each chapter's main conceptual focus:

Chapter 2: Words

Texts are both works of literature that can be enjoyed wholly and fully in a literary sense, and also are symbolic as in the work they perform within theatrical as opposed to filmic contexts. The world of a play or performance text becomes realized in production as an act of interpretation.

Words written for the page do the work of telling stories, but words written for performance move beyond narrative storytelling as they paint pictures, create worlds, and offer audiences a three-dimensional and multi-sensory experience of being in time and space together. Performers and their scripts are in the business of conjuring worlds in a multi-dimensional plane, not only a meeting but also a disjuncture in time and space. This disjuncture (between the performed time of the play or performance world—i.e., a year on stage is not equal to a year of performance; even a single rotation of the sun in Aristotle's conception of drama is not often replicated on stage) offers an opening to the symbolic world in which audiences experience an alteration to reality and can suspend the laws of their everyday lives in favour of a shared ritualised experience. This ritualised experience is never the same twice, changing according to context (i.e., audience, location, time, etc.) and also according to form (i.e., the world of a solo performance or agit prop performance in the public sphere is not the same as a well-made play performance).

As a result of such changeable conditions, the relationship between the writer of performance, the performer, the character, and the audience member exists in (and is affected by) this temporal and physical distance. For this reason, writing for performance is both more ephemeral than most other creative texts, and more fixed than most performance artefacts or tools, and so the 'performance text' is always a liminal document, a tool that exists for purposes other than its tangible state and any other kind of book reader. As a symbolic representation of a three-dimensional world and event, performance texts are both material and symbolic, and their purposes are always shared collaborative and multiple.

The work of the performance text is in animating symbolism. The words that comprise a performance text function in a symbolic register and always in relationship with bodies and things and space and time. So while the role of words in performance and performance texts might be central, words are also marginal. As we show in the second chapter, embodiment remains at the heart of performance, and words are the interlocutor between the language of bodies, the animation of things and the audience's reception or collaboration in meaning-making in the space of performance.

If performance is a medium of symbolism, then writing for performance is always both embodied and symbolic work. Performance (and its writing) is never a real rendering of life (even when it is realistic, as in the context of realism or naturalism) because:

• Time is collapsed
• Actions stand for something larger

- There is a difference between the prop, which is symbolic and objects which are things-in-themselves
- Characters are representative of themes/ideas and are more than individual selves/subjectivities or particular experiences and points of view
- The emotional tone or trajectory of the text is also greater than the experience of individual characters (i.e., selves/subjectivities)
- Context and historic specificity are less defined; there is a pull toward the universal.

Chapter Two opens up a discussion of how language and words facilitate the work of performance—focusing not on how words are a *destination* in that work, but rather on how words are a *tool* along the road toward embodiment.

Chapter 3: Bodies

Chapter Three considers the primacy of the body and embodiment in performance and helps readers to understand its utilitarian and symbolic relationship to words, to things, and to space and time.

Orality is an aspect of embodiment; in performance, there are never just words floating alone in air. Performance texts must be 'spoken'; they must be interpreted for the hearer/viewer and embodied in voice, sound, rhythm, timbre, and tone of voice (something might make sense on the page that doesn't make sense for the stage). In performance contexts and in relation to performance texts, words serve a physical and material form and function. They exist in time, in space, in rhythm and timbre. Words join the body of the performer with the ears and eyes of the audience in a relational way that is immediate, confrontative, and demonstrative. Performance texts and their performers use words as a relational offering, not a solitary act, not an abstract symbol. Writing for performance is of course still beautiful writing, but it is writing that becomes itself—becomes beautiful or searing or transcendent in the mouths of the performers.

Embodiment for performing bodies exists and is enacted in space and time, including both virtual and 'live' spaces. Embodiment as performed involves a pact/contract with the audience. From the experience of co-habiting within the performance space, the words of the performer create an altered or heightened world into which the audience member is invited. While this book explores the ways in which liveness can be experienced both online and offline, we focus primarily on the level of risk and responsibility demanded of both performers and audience members in embodied performance contexts, in which the performance pivots on the bodies-sharing-space experience of live performance. To co-inhabit a performance space, this sense of risk and responsibility is heightened for both the performer and, in some forms, for the audience. The performer is co-present with the audience in live spaces, thus changing the investment of the delivery and reception—the co-creation—of the performance (Spry, 2011). Such investments occur differently in virtual spaces; indeed the level of risk and responsibility are utterly different in online and offline spaces. This chapter considers the powerfully diverse and various forms of embodiment: speaking and moving, silent embodiment, and virtual embodiment, all suggesting myriad other ways in which the exchange of performance continues to demand new and other forms of embodiment. All carry with them different advantages and limitations, as this chapter points out.

Chapter 4: Things

Chapter Four considers how the symbols of performance (objects or things) are themselves performative, as well as how performance is made of and in relation to things. Semiotics—the study of signs and symbols in/as a process of representation—teaches us to pay attention to ways in which words themselves can be considered symbols, signs, and tools with wills and lives of their own, in relation to and separate from their human counterparts. Here, texts are things with lives and wills of their own, in relation to and separate from their human counterparts. In this view, the 'thingness' of texts means that they can show us how things do or don't make sense in ways that don't neatly line up with ideas about the well-made play, plot and character, and depicting a world to an audience. Instead, the thingness of texts insists that writing for performance is a way of questioning and constructing an(other) view of the world. Thus beyond their representational and symbolic value, words, things, and embodiments work together in performance to bring to life meaning. This chapter explores this interrelationship while focusing on the potential for performing things to extend and enrich what words, bodies, and spaces offer audiences and to make things 'mean' differently.

The chapter focuses on the work of avant-garde writers and artists such as Dadist Trstian Tzara and experimental novelist Gertrude Stein who searched for other ways of telling stories that questioned the modern logics of rationalism, progress, and capitalism in the wake of the first and second world wars. These artists and writers ask us to pay attention to how we make the raw material of language mean *differently* through the practice of collage. Collage approaches to writing for performance combine source materials from one context (words, images, three-dimensional objects, bodies, sounds, projections, etc.) and place them in relation to another context. Each element in a collage refers at once to an external reality and re-imagines or re-verses the meanings previously assigned to that reality through the techniques of doubleness (the lives of things both inside and outside the performance), juxtaposition (placing different things in relation to one another) and repetition (reiteration that emphasizes the multiple and diverse relationships among the elements of any collage).

The chapter includes exemplars of writing for performance using collage techniques and offers readers several approaches for/writing exercises to using collage methods in their own writing.

Chapter 5: Spaces

Chapter Five takes our discussion of the primacy of the performing body and embodiment and the aliveness and 'thingness' of words and text into a consideration of their relationship to space. The chapter begins with the writing spaces those who write for performance create for themselves. Most writers talk specifically about the spaces they need in which to make work (like any other maker). Some writers have strict environmental requirements, using or programming the space around them strategically, as an immersive environment, which assists them in creating the world that is part or context for the world they are creating. Other writers listen to music that they find evocative for either the specific piece they are writing, or for unlocking their 'writing mind' in general. Still others alter their spaces physically, by writing in alternative private spaces (like offices or writers' rooms) or public spaces (writers like Patti Smith who prefer to write in cafes), or other specific environments such as trains.

This chapter also looks critically at the way the performance writer must approach the work of writing with a consideration of space. Here, space is seen as a collaborator in writing for performance—that is, to enter a performance space is to enter a process of writing, one in which writers, performers, and audiences leave impressions on the space and the space leaves impressions on writers, performers, and audiences. Space also asks us to take into account the environment of the performance. What is the performance space itself like, and what context does that performance space inhabit? If you are writing a performance text for performance in a traditional theatre, the work will be different if performed in a theatre on Broadway versus a theatre in a back alley in Taipei, versus a university black box theatre in Dehli. If the text you are writing is intended as a guide for a more generative, improvisational performance in a non-traditional performance space such as a train platform in Edinburgh, or a living room in Florence, or a beach in Thailand, what are the considerations that you as a performance writer must keep in mind for your work to be realised in a way that feels complete, despite (or because of) these diverse settings and spaces? Additionally, the body performs in space and time, whether that performance occurs online or offline. Indeed, more and more often, the performing body incorporates a relationship with video and online and digital others (times, spaces, things). Whether it is a live performance that incorporates video, or a performance experienced online, or a live performance created or disseminated in online spaces, the performance writer can no longer speak of performance spaces as solely in-person spaces.

Finally, the chapter asks readers to consider how the performance text itself is a space, or environment in which performance occurs. In other words, how do writers create texts that are or become material and corporeal spaces in performance? The chapter considers the writing spaces, performance spaces, and texts as spaces through the work of a number of exemplars and offers readers a series of writing exercises and prompts for writing space.

Chapter 6: Rehearsing/Devising

Chapter Six offers readers a brief overview of rehearsing and devising processes. As we note above, a book about writing performance would not be complete without a consideration of these processes; however, it is beyond the scope of this text to provide an in-depth treatment of rehearsing and devising (that would the another book altogether and there are many fine examples of such texts). In this chapter we chart those processes across the lifespan of a performance that began as in-depth research interviews, moved into a workshop-devised interactive performance (*Out/In Front: Teaching Change*), and took new life as a (further devised and) scripted play for theatre (*Heavier Than Air*). We discuss the origins of the research, writing, devising, and performance project, particularly decisions we made about the message we wanted to convey with the work and how to best honour the words and lived experiences of the interviewees on which the play is based, while making an interactive and participatory performance. We share some of the original interview transcripts so readers can see how they changed in order to create the performance, along with our devising and thinking process as we incorporated feedback during both rehearsals and revising over the initial development of the play.

Chapter 7: Revising/Performing

In Chapter Seven we continue our consideration of the text-to-performance process, following the transition the *Out/In Front* play from an in-process text-based performance presented in the round to *Heavier Than Air*, a fully-produced performance work that makes use of text, embodiments, space, and sound. In particular, we offer readers a discussion of how considerations of performance space altered the staging and performer-audience encounter and how such considerations are integrally tied to not only the development of the performance text per se, but to the larger context and politic of the work.

Chapter 8: Beginnings, Again

What does it mean to offer readers a concluding chapter called "Beginnings"? Indeed, how does any of us ever get started? So many lists of 'ways in' serve to stymie those to whom they do not speak, who feel that what they are doing is 'wrong' and who, in looking for validation, end up in greater self-doubt. Doing both a Bachelors and Masters degrees in Dramatic Writing at NYU taught Anne two simple but important things:

1. You can't teach someone to write. You can teach form.
2. There is no one way of doing things, despite a pervasive desire for formulae.

Ultimately most of Anne's professors (some of them the most successful writers for film, television, and the American theatre) taught her that the only important thing is that you write. Some of us do it every day, some in intense spurts, some painfully, some joyfully. Success comes as a result of many different practices, as does 'failure'. Yet at the end of the day, the only thing a writer can control is getting words on the page, and to be a writer you must ultimately find a way to do so, in whatever ways work for you. That is all.

WORDS

BOOKS AND MAPS

Writing for performance is different than other forms of writing, in that it magically accomplishes a dual function: performance scripts are both literary works—that is, they are meant to be read—and performative artefacts, written with their ultimate performance in mind. One of the reasons Anne has always preferred playwriting and performance writing over prose is due to the economy of language in performance scripts. She loved to write primarily for the rhythms and cadences of peoples' language, how they spoke, what that revealed about them. Not just the words they chose, but the way they organised those words, ordered them, metered them, repeated them. Sometimes avoided them. From the age of four, she was trained in the performance and theory of piano. Her later love of performance writing seemed as much tied to this musical beginning as it did to a love of language and words. That's why, even though she enjoyed writing stories and ultimately a novel, she chose instead to focus on performance writing because she could do away with all the descriptive (and sometimes flowery) prose that made her impatient as a reader—she always wanted to skip the 'description' and get to the 'action'. Writing for performance is, in some ways, this orientation exactly—after brief attention to the 'setting' at the opening of a performance script, the text is solely focused on action and dialogue. In fact, dialogue itself becomes the action as we watch characters do battle with words and silences.

In a very tangible way, performance texts are both works of literature which can be enjoyed wholly and fully in a literary sense (read like a book), and also maps for creating or recalling or recreating a performance (instructions for getting somewhere, or indeed, for getting lost). For some performance writers, like playwrights and performers such as Anna Deavere Smith (who draws the dialogue for her performances from interview transcripts), the playscript is an exact reproduction of the performance, rendered in words. That is, the dialogue spoken, the stage directions that describe where the performance occurs, and the setting in which the action takes place and instruct how and when characters speak and to whom, are all detailed in the text. The world of a play or performance text becomes realized in production as an act of interpretation. However, for other performance writers, performance texts serve as guideposts or blueprints for what might be done or said on stage.

THE VOICE OF A PERFORMANCE TEXT

Sometimes, it's hard to tell on the page how a play or performance script might sound 'on its feet' (a phrase for describing how a play or performance looks and sounds once onstage). The ability to 'hear' the 'voice' of a play is at the heart of the work of *dramaturgs* (German term for 'script doctor'), *literary managers* (script experts employed by theatre companies), *literary agents* (in theatre and film) and *play development* experts. According to these literary midwives, finding the *voice* of a performance script is a central task of playwrights, dramaturgs, and the directors with whom they work (Harris, 2014).

But what is *voice* in a performance text, and is it different than the voice of a novel, or a painting, or a poem? There is no one answer to this question, but in this book we offer readers some examples of what voice looks, sounds, and feels like when writing for performance. If the performance piece is a public space performance that does not rely upon a theatre (or any sort of seated audience), does not conform to well-made play constraints, and expects to be moving and audible, that voice must be one that reaches out and captures people in their everyday lives. It must be accessible, distinct, and compelling. What kind of performance story 'catches' an audience's attention? One reason why we both love the form of performance writing known as performance poetry (sometimes called spoken word or slam poetry in a competitive context) is because of the immediacy of *voice*. In this form, and because these performances often take place in cafes, bars, and other immediate and hybrid spaces, the voice of the performer must be intense, and the story or message—often a political or social critique—must be clear. Audiences at performance poetry events are like television viewers with unlimited channels and a remote in hand: they are impatient and demanding; they want the performer to grab them by the throat and not let go. There is no time for complicated set ups or exposition. They get in, they grab us with their theatrical voice (often angry, passionate, or despairing), and they start running, urging us to hurry up and follow along (or be left behind).

WORDS AND BODIES

And while, as we said in Chapter One, performers and their texts are in the business of conjuring worlds out of air, and therefore opening us to the symbolic, today's performance contexts have been profoundly impacted by digital media and information overload. We are more used to the virtual, less concerned with essentialising questions of 'real' versus 'abstract' or 'live' and 'virtual' because we know that virtual worlds in both online *and* offline situations can be equally compelling or equally dead. What audiences of live performance *are* demanding about is being moved, affected, and viscerally and visually impacted. They demand a multisensory experience. So even though we are talking about writing *words* for performance, remember that those words are always accompanied by bodies that deliver them—with sweat, movement, smells, sights, and sounds—and the profoundly human experience of being just close enough to touch—almost. Most often, live performance does hinge upon words, it's true. But those words are coming out of a fragile human mouth, from a face contorted by the passions of that dialogue, with eyes staring into your own, asking to be met. Writing for performance always implies the desire to be met as bodies in time and space. And this was true as much in the time of Aristotle and Greek tragedies as it is today. Whether those performances and stories are told around a fire, from the lip of a proscenium stage, or in the middle of New York City's Grand Central Station as part of a flashmob or an Occupy rally, we continue to have a 'need to tell' and to listen to others' stories.

If, as we have said, the work of the performance text is in animating symbolism, it is equally important in reminding audiences of the symbolic aspects of our animated lives and bodies. It is all too easy, especially today, to forget the symbolic and spiritual dimension of our lived experiences and indeed our bodies. In the midst of a seemingly global obsession with reality television—and perhaps more so because of this—we continue to crave the symbolic, to find meaning in the mundane. Words, as Jacques Derrida (1998) tells us, inhabit the realm of the symbolic. If performance is a medium of symbolism, then writing for performance is always both embodied and symbolic work. Words are, as we have said, tools that facilitate the work of performance, not a destination in and of themselves.

WORDS AND ACTIONS

Words help construct the plot of a performance: we know what happened largely because the characters *tell* us it happened. Aristotle's first principle of drama is 'plot', and while plot as he defines it is 'action' and not 'narrative', words themselves are action/active. As teachers of performance writing, we advise students to, 'show, don't tell.' Aristotle says that plot is the 'arrangement of the incidents', not the story itself. In other words, the plot is the structure of actions, not dialogue or descriptions or recountings. However, the fourth principle of drama is 'diction' or 'the expression of the meaning in words', in which his discussion is most concerned with metaphor. Aristotle's specificity can still be seen today in the need for good dramatists to synthesise, create dramatic layers, and achieve parallelism, or the ability "to make good metaphors implies an eye for resemblances" (Aristotle in *Poetics*, Part XXII, n.p.). Sometimes these resemblances create their own dramatic action and reaction onstage and form the basis for the layering of relationships and repercussions that make good theatre, regardless of the historical moment.

The words a writer uses to construct a performance text are also materially alive, and not only representative. New materialist scholars, for example, propose new relationships between authors and texts; relationships that avoid 'us' and 'them' differences and that place authors in outsider positions to their 'inanimate' scripts. Rather, Kaisa Kurikka (2012) finds more interest in the matter, functions, and effects of words, moving us beyond static representations and reductive notions of what a text can and cannot do, or what it is or is not. It also allows for a refocus from the author as a singular person who writes a singular work into what Kurikka calls a "conceptual persona" (p. 121), following Gilles Deleuze and Felix Guattari (1988). Such a view draws on the social domain of language in which "two formalizations are encountered: one of content and one of expression; one of the seeable and one of the sayable. Each has a form and a substance—because of this the relationship between them is not representationalist" (Kurikka, 2012, pp. 117–118). For a playwright like Samuel Beckett, the relationship between the seeable and the sayable—between waiting and speaking—can both be a meditation on the failure of language as much as the absurdity of 'performance'.

In *Waiting for Godot*, Beckett masterfully uses not only the content and materiality of words, but also their pacing. This classic absurdist play (plays that take the form of human response to a world without meaning) moves between long silences and circular action to moments in which language pours out of the characters in torrents of words, an experience for audiences of an almost-material waterfall of language in which despair and terror can be found. In Beckett, word and action dance together to make the drama. "If the main resource of twentieth-century directors was to exploit discontinuities, to open up a space for meaning to emerge between word and action, then they found that Beckett had trumped them at their own game" (Bradby, 2001, p. 138). Another beautiful way of thinking of his important text is that "without an ounce of literature—I mean self-conscious literature—Samuel Beckett gives us a profoundly poetic work" (p. 54), one in which "the musical quality of the play and the way that the actions, as well as the words and silence, were composed [was] a kind of concrete poetry" (p. 100). We agree that there is absolute difference between the word written to be read and the word written to be performed or verbalized, yet the work these words do varies between genre, era, and cultural and historical context.

In the following exemplars, consider how words are at once fluid, conceptual, and interwoven. The worlds these words create are both material and relational; they serve as multisensory pivots and provocateurs as they work together toward the creation of texts for performing.

EXEMPLAR ONE: *A DYKE IS NOT A DAM*

Anne has written two plays using a body of music from two different artists: she wrote the full-length play *Endsville* from the songs of Frank Sinatra, and she wrote a one-act play titled *A Dyke is Not a Dam* from the songs of Bette Midler. Here we will draw from the latter. Anne wrote and produced this one-act play about lesbian life in an attempt to represent the diversity of lesbian and queer female life she felt was missing in the popular theatre at that time. She was immersed in a vibrant gay theatre scene that was reeling from the decimation of the AIDS epidemic, but still had a long way to go in representing a wide range of lesbian experiences. In this collage text, she set herself the task of using Bette Midler's songbook (typically associated with gay men) as a provocation for a series of monologues and dialogues and small group scenes. The full work was about an hour long, and could be performed as a cabaret work, could be mounted as a full theatre production, or could be separated into individual monologues/scenes for short-form presentation. Each scene/piece was written after listening to the Midler songs and hearing the 'voice' of a character, who then 'told' Anne the story evokes emotionally in the listener by that song. This kind of devising process offers nearly endless possibilities, as songs are interpretive and multiple performance pieces could of course be written to even the same song or musical provocation.

Anne has presented these monologues and scenes in several festivals and conferences, and the Midler soundtrack is always as pivotal to the effect and mood as are the words. The following monologue, 'Tragedy', is indirectly about the character's coming out experience, set against the loss of her brother. It highlights the pain of family complexities for the queer family member, and this piece grows directly out of *Tragedy's* melody and lyrics.

Tragedy
(to Bette Midler's *Tragedy)*

Shelly.

In 1984 my brother shot himself in a men's room in Manhattan.
It was the wrong room.
He was just a boy.
I was sixteen years old,
and I can't write about it
right
enough
my love, my love, my love was this boy
with him i travelled
in my mind.
He saved me
from less safe days
and brothers
(like smoke from a fire
i love love loved him…).

It was autumn,
the most beautiful time
in my town
with colors of every kind
every shade
you can dream
and when I tell them about Michael it still sounds empty
it still sounds false, but
when i came out i went to his gravestone
in an ugly little cemetery near a church i had
long-since abandoned
and came out to him
and he understood about having to do
what will save you.
or not.

I brought a six-pack of Bud and a soft-pack of Kents,
his old brand,
and i told him the whole story
of me, my feelings, i sang a song.
Because isn't loving a little like dying?
And i regretted that he could not
tell me more.
Big brothers are supposed to
be there.
He's there.
He's here.

WRITING EXERCISE ONE: CREATING CHARACTER FROM MUSIC

A common creative writing exercise uses music to set an ambience or scene in which the writer can play out the action intended. Music in this case can show the reader or audience the tone of the scene, not unlike other atmospheric elements such as weather, colours, or props. However, in this exercise we use music to help inform and build characters, as Anne did above.

1. Choose three very different pieces of music.
2. Play the first piece and free write throughout the piece, using only the first person ("I"). Let this first character writing be about the kind of person the music is (i.e., "I love this piece because it reminds me of my grandmother who was an arctic explorer in the 1930s and we used to sit on her porch in southern Indiana and she would tell me these stories…").
3. Play the second piece and free write in the first person again, but this time telling a story about something incredible this person has observed that day (i.e., "God I wish he would turn off that music because even if I get ahold of someone at the school I will not be able to hear them and if they don't get someone down here right away these kids are going to kill themselves on that highway!"). So this is still a monologue in the first person, but more observational than reflective.
4. Play the third piece and write a dialogue between one of the first two characters and your four-year-old self. What do you (as that four year old) want to say? Are they listening to you? How does this piece of music make your four-year-old self feel and why is today the day that your four-year-old self is going to try to be heard?
5. You now have three characters informed by three different styles of music. You can play with these characters and moods crashing against each other

in various ways. You can also write different versions of each character, including the elderly version, the male/female/genderqueer version, the wealthy version, the person who lives in poverty version, or the version written by the singer/composer of those pieces of music. There are many ways to use the provocation. Lastly, try using the lyrics (if you have any) themselves as dialogue and see where they take you.

EXEMPLAR TWO: *LEAVE TO STAY*

This exemplar is a multi-layered piece written and performed by Anne on commission by the Sydney Mardi Gras (LGBTIQ festival) in the early 2000s. While she was glad to be able to share some of her fictionalised 'queer immigration' story (based on her experiences emigrating to Australia from the USA), Anne was extremely concerned about Australia's treatment of asylum seekers and refugees, an issue still continuing today and more critically condemned by the United Nations than it was then. Anne looked for a way to comment on the political injustice of what was happening to asylum seekers while still fulfilling her commission to present a 'queer' performance piece. A foreshortened version of the piece she presented is below. This text interweaves writing on the themes of queer identity, family, racism, immigration, and refugee abuses. It is included here as an exemplar of writing to a current issue or political situation, leveraging personal narrative with cultural contexts or what some writers call performance autoethnography. While you read this performance piece, notice Anne's performance notes to herself for emphasis while rehearsing/performing.

Leave to Stay

She wears me like a badge.
she secretly turns me over, on her tongue.

The thought of me makes her **mouth** water
it floods her so she has to
swallow, to keep from choking.
so much water it runs bitter, caustic,
and she loves that too.
for once, finally, she can taste something.

I'm one of her 'projects'.
She loves me because i'm **white**
middle class, and she loves me in some sick way **because**

—not in **spite** of but BECAUSE—i'm American.
I'm the way it was **always** supposed to be.

***

The woman in question
the woman to whom I refer
is a representative of the minister for immigration.
She's a hot little number, she's paid her dues.
She never wanted to live in Darwin, but you have to make these sacrifices
to get ahead.
You see, she wants a better life for herself and her kids.

***

My application was held up by the Timorese problem.
She used to tell me, my representative,
that she regretted it,
and she was tired,
but I mustn't worry.
She'd see to me.
She'd call me again as soon as there was any news.

***

Which raised the question of why someone in her position
would be so pleasant, so chummy,
to someone in mine.
as a lesbian, I wasn't used to it.
It made me suspicious.

***

Dear Immigration:

To Whom It May Concern:

I am writing to confirm that my daughter, Lola Palatska, has indeed deserted her family in America as she says she has. She thinks she's in love with some Australian lawyer and
far be it from me to tell her otherwise *[fast!]*
(not to mention it's a **woman** lawyer, but we're not allowed to argue THAT one anymore, **so** i'm trying to be happy it's not a drug addict).
She never listened to me anyhow.

I hope she'll be very happy while her father and mother who have toiled for her, suffered for her, and given up the best years of their lives sit familyless and alone somewhere in America waiting for the phone to ring. (which it never does).

I hope if you believe her and give her residency she'll be **satisfied**.
And then maybe the mystery will lose it's flavour
and she'll snap out of this ridiculous delusion
that she wants to live somewhere other than the United States of America. God forbid.
You can't understand kids these days.
Lola's father nearly killed himself fighting for this great land of ours,
and now his own daughter walks away from it. Go figure.
Good luck to you, maybe you can do more with her than I could.
She's not a bad girl once you get to know her.

With warm regards,

Mrs. Estelle Palatska
Eastern Parkway,
Brooklyn, New York

***

[fast]
We sent in 375 pages of supporting documentation:
bank statements, photos of our holidays to Paris, New York, the great ocean road.
mortgage accounts, movie tickets, letters from the town council,
postcards from abroad, entry stubs from Graceland. We had it all.
photocopied to perfection, signed by the notary.

Some days I thank god that Margaret's a lawyer, other days I don't.
She likes to tell people that doctors shouldn't treat their own families, that
she lost perspective on our case.
Which she did.
But today's a day it's a good thing to have a lawyer in the family.
Today's the interview.

***

For once, Margaret's sound asleep,
but tonight I'm wide awake.

Besides that, my jaw hurts.
I've recently realised that I clench my **teeth** when I sleep.
My ex-lover wasn't surprised:
that's nothing new, she said, vindicated to know
that my clenching was not just the result of
the stressful love affair with her.
I've always been a stressy girl. I call it hypervigilance, ever since I did my
class on 'overcoming overwhelm' at the New York open centre ten years ago?
I have **insight** into my stress now.
it's a product of the orphanage. i'm convinced.
every abandoned child is hypervigilant.
and abandoned children who grow up in violent homes are doubly hyper-vigilant,
and **Americans** are hyper-vigilant by **birth**, so that leaves me…
extremely, constantly, culturally hyper-viligilant.
hyper-hyper-vigilant.

***

Dear Director of Immigration and Multicultural Affairs:
G'day.
I am writing to support the application of my friends Lola and Margaret, who are **definitely** lezzos. You should have seen them last Mardi Gras. Nobody who is not a dyke would act like that. I'm a tour guide, so my **word** is my **business**. You've got my word that those two are about as queer as a three dollar note. Furthermore, they love each other to pieces. I can give examples if you request. Feel free to ring me. Or better yet, come on down to the Alice, and I'll take you out on a private tour for a re-enactment.
Yours Sincerely,
Shazza Delaney

***

A blessing of this techno age
is the ability to travel widely and easily.
Cheaply, at least in dollars.
It's both the blessing and the curse.

29

***

I can, if and when I get sick enough of my life as it is
pick up and go.
and if that place gets boring or confronting enough
I can pick and go again.
in fact, I've discovered I can do this as many times as it
takes to stay comfortable.
But, like alcohol,
there is a point at which the equation starts to work backwards.
It's one of those naturally-occurring fractions of nature:
it starts out costing zero percent of the whole.
Then the number above the line starts to grow,
while the number below the line starts to shrink,
and all of a sudden you wake up one morning
and realize you can
no longer adequately **reinvent** yourself
because you don't know who you are to begin with.
You don't remember where you **started**.
There is nothing left of the old **you** to jump off **from**.

***

To Whom It May Concern at the Department of Immigration and Home-Wrecking:

I regret to inform you that my husband, Stanley Palatska, passed away last Tuesday. I know Lola is supposed to stay in that god-forsaken country until **you** get around to making up your mind whether or not you want her, but could you please let her out to come home to the funeral?
Not that it isn't a case of too little too late, but in this country we do have a tradition of daughters caring about their fathers.
Furthermore, I have it on good authority that Mr. Palatska has left instructions in his will that you are to nationalise my daughter, at your earliest convenience. Personally, I think he just didn't want her coming back harassing **me**. But you know he was a bit of a traveller, Mr. Palatska, from his Navy days, and he always believed in trying to improve yourself. So I've been thinking since last Tuesday that it may be God's will for Lola to stay in the land Down Below.

I've received other messages from God; in fact I'm quite well-known in Flatbush for this gift. So I suggest you read the writing on the wall and
a) let Lola come home for the funeral but
b) let her stay there for the rest of her life if that is what she so desires.

PS – if you'd like a little tchotchke from Brooklyn, I'd be happy to send one back with Lola. Just let her know.

Good luck and Happy Holidays,
Mrs. Estelle Palatska,
Eastern Parkway,
Brooklyn, New York

***

I was born to certain parents, with certain siblings,
in a particular place and time, and so for all intents and purposes
these are my people. This is the landscape of my heart.
I may wish to leave them.
I may hate their guts.
But my earliest childhood memories are impregnated here.
In my mind. In my heart. In my blood.
Irrevocable.
My people become the only ones who Know The Whole Story of Me.
This becomes a more precious commodity
as life ebbs away.
My father knew this.

***

He came from West Texas to Death Valley.
He thought they were the same, because they looked the same.
He was fooled.
He thought he was getting a new life.
Instead, he lived with ghosts from the age of thirty instead of
from the age of seventy.
He had a wide circle of friends—in his mind.
He travelled widely—in dreams.
There was no difference between his dead and his living –
everyone who was important to him was **gone**.
If not literally, then geographically.

CHAPTER 2

And rather than help to go home on visits,
it was like a great tear,
a great gaping tract of scar tissue up his
guts, across his belly, through his heart—
and every time he **saw** or **spoke** or **held** or listened to someone from **home**,
this great wound split open and threatened to consume him.
So he began to leave it further and further behind.
And the truth was that even before he had left West Texas
his heart was already on this path,
because he had never known his people,
being an orphan.
He had never known the heartbeat that he listened to in the womb
had never heard the laugh of his first days
had never gazed into a face like his own
and so even before he chose exile, he had **been** exiled.
The geographical move just confirmed and externalised what he
had felt for so long inside.
He was a stranger in his own land.
And then a stranger in a strange land.
Finally he lived so much in his head
that he would look around at the rest of us:
his wife, his children, his neighbors and friends,
with a look of **utter incomprehension**.
And although it looked to us like contempt
I began to know that it was really fear.
He didn't know how he'd arrived in this place.
He didn't know where he was, nor who **we** were.
Nothing looked familiar.
I have acquired the same view
from my window. On sleepless nights.

***

This incessant desire to renew, if only we could see it for what it is,
could actually be quite useful.
That's where immigrants have it over everyone else.
Immigrants **know** how much is lost in this process,
The rest of you don't care until it's too late.
You think you still will find your one true love.

You really do think there are differences between people.
But immigrants know this is not true.
Immigrants know that all people are only as different as
circumstance:

***

We come into a strange land alone,
in a mystical and mysterious manner.
We know not how we arrive, nor when and how we will depart.
We grow accostomed to some **things** and some **faces**,
but by and by they leave or change or die,
and we are reminded that we are just visitors here.
And our stay is short and tenuous.

***

Margaret is waking up now.
I can hear her stirring.
It'll be time to shower, dress, spray, powder,
make-up, moisturize,
and go.
And in one moment, the interviewer will
decide 'my fate'.
We met her once before:
In the first round.
She was informal, in slacks and shirt sleeves,
down from Darwin on the 8:50 Ansett then.
We sat around the pool drinking coffees.
She was impressed we wore frocks.
We don't always, said Margaret, before I kicked her under the table.
She was Territory casual.
Let's hope she is today.
Let's hope she sees us as one of Us, not one of Them.
It's a fine line
and changing all the time.
Yesterday, before the boats began arriving, queers were one of **Them**.
Timing is everything. *[smiles]*
Now, I'm the kind of applicant a girl could make a career on.
I'm easy.
And if she's in a good mood,

33

if she got laid last night
if she had breakfast
if she's got a generous expense account for the trip,
perhaps I'll be one of Us
and she'll grant me
leave to stay.

***

She loves me, she loves me not. *[wry]*
If not...
I'll start again.
Because, in my case, I can.

We have included this examplar to draw attention to the ways words alone as performance tools can vividly convey not only stories and events, but places, smells, sights, and multiple voices. What did you think while reading the monologue? Did you wonder if the performer changed her voice when performing as Mrs. Estelle Palatska? Did you find the shift between the 'queering' of the immigration officer and the 'guilt' of Mrs Palatska difficult or jarring? Did you identify more with one of these characters than the others? Spoken word or monologue performances like these open up word-based performative possibilities for the writer and performer both, enjoying the slippage between characters at times.

WRITING EXERCISE TWO: CREATING CHARACTER FROM A NEWS ITEM

Take an article from a local newspaper. Do not take a news item off the Internet, because these news items are compromised in two ways: they are often untrue and taken out of context, and then are almost never YOUR community. This exercise is about writing about your people, your place, your issue.

1. So go down the street, find a bodega, a milk bar, a convenience store, or a 7-Eleven and buy a newspaper. Any newspaper. There is also the important tactile aspect of writing, and writing in response to things that are happening in your immediate world involves actually getting your hands dirty. Remember (if you can) what it feels like to have your fingers smeared with newsprint? Go do it. You will feel more connected to the dirty issue once your hands are dirty too.

2. Flip through the paper. Find something that catches your eye. It doesn't have to be something you feel sympathetic about, in fact sometimes this is an obstacle to good writing. Go find something that catches your writer's eye and then go get a pair of scissors out of your office or kitchen draw or wherever and cut that thing out of there.

3. Tape it up, pin it up, put some bubble gum on it but get it UP, on the wall, in front of your eyes. Then stare at it for a while until it starts to shape-shift. Stare at it until you hear voices. Stare at it until you are so irritated, disgusted, heartbroken or in love that you just HAVE to write something.

4. Write it in the first person, always the first person. Do not stop to think about it, do not editorialise. It's okay to be biased. People are biased, characters are biased, and good writing for theatre is always (at least for a while) biased, emotive, and invested. Write that monologue. Forget about it as an 'issue' (which has no soul), but strive to stay connected to it as a STORY, someone's story that has within it unbearable injustice. And then set out to tell this injustice to someone who is either antagonistic to it, or has never heard a word about it. Bring them in, don't preach.

5. Read it out loud. Does it make you cry or angry? If not, start over and repeat steps 1–4.

WORDS AND...

Words form and often take centre stage in writing for performance. They are at once works of literature to be read and enjoyed on the page and also works that are intended to be voiced, embodied, and experienced on the stage. As we noted in the opening of this chapter, while writing for performance is certainly a practice that (often) begins with words, words are not separate or distinct from the bodies that write, speak, and inhabit them. In Chapter Three, we consider the relationship of words to these bodies.

BODIES

BODIES CARRY (THE PERFORMANCE) WORD

As we noted in Chapter One, this chapter shifts our attention toward the primacy of the body and embodiment in performance, and to understanding its practical relationship to words, to things, and to time and spaces. Performance scholar Philip Auslander argues that theatre offers audiences "a fuller sensory experience than mediatized performances" (Auslander, 1999, p. 55). In contrast, performance artist Helen Paris claims that mediatized performance is not *less* multisensory than live performance, but only differently so. Her disagreement with Auslander's claims pivot, for her, on *smell*. Wherever you see the role of live performance on the virtual/live continuum, the visceral intensity and multisensory richness of live performance—whether it's smell, touch, or emotional intensity—is one of its greatest assets.

When writing for performance, spoken words become an extension of the body; they are never *just words* floating in air. In other words, bodies carry the performance word (Jones, 1998). This means that language in performance is enacted in relationship to bodies—the performer's and the audience's. Words join the body of the performer with the ears, eyes, noses, and bodies the audience in ways that can be felt, heard, and seen. These words must be interpreted for the hearer/viewer and embodied in voice, sound, rhythm, timbre, and tone of voice, and words that might make sense on the page might not, in the end, make sense for the stage.

The body of a live performer means that the work is co-created with the audience in live spaces, whether online or offline (Spry, 2011). Embodiment involves a pact/contract between the performer(s) and the audience, one in which the performer(s) create an altered or heightened world into which the audience member is invited. To cohabit a performance space, whether online or offline (or a combination of the two, as is increasingly popular in performance), risk and responsibility are demanded of the performer and of the audience. Performance is characterised by the presence (risk) of the body. Live and virtual embodiments are both certainly still embodiments; each requiring presence and relational risk, though the body is differently implicated in each. This is what makes performance (unlike film) unique each time a work is performed, whether it is improvisational or scripted. This chapter considers some of the diverse and various forms of embodiment in performance and how these bodies impact, alter, and generate performance writing in different ways.

(WRITING FOR) SPEAKING AND MOVING

…I thought that a puppet was a sign that somewhere in my mind, something believed in souls and sprites, gods and goblins, since puppets manifest externally and materially the *mode of being* of imaginary spirits; the whole concept resting on the idea of enchanted matter. Similar considerations can be made about theater, opera and other forms of embodiment of characters. Each of these are about different types of embodiment, but in some way they seem related to the profound and ancient notions of souls (gods or the dead, or mythic or legendary characters) speaking through human beings, reminding of shamanic possession (psychokinetic control by a spiritual being). My point here is … to show that these forms do have meaning, that they actualize certain conceptions (most often unconscious) and are significant in terms of our own ways of being. (Boutet, 2012, pp. 34–35)

What does it mean to write for a body that moves and speaks? It means acknowledging firstly that all bodies move and speak in different ways. Indeed, the art form of acting is a coming-to-know more explicitly how one's body moves and speaks. But the body of a performer moves and speaks in a range of publics. That is, the body does not perform if it performs alone. Like the old adage, 'if a tree falls in the forest and there is no one there to hear it fall, does it make a sound?', the work of a performing body is relational. Of course, performance does not always include speaking and moving. Some performance artists, including Marina Abramovic and her longtime performance artist partner Ulay (Uwe Laysiepen) have extended the complexity of performances that include neither moving nor speaking, and they are no less powerful. Indeed, even in their stillness they comment on speaking and moving (see http://www.openculture.com/2013/12/artist-marina-abramovic-former-lover-ulay-reunite.html).

Like Danielle Boutet above, our point is to not only show that there are many different *forms* of writing for performance, but also to underscore that there are particular and different meanings attached to those forms. When writing for speaking and moving performers/performances, it is important to remember that words can easily take priority as the primary mode of communication. It is the job of the writer (initially) to ensure this does not happen, balancing the speaking *and* the moving of the performer's body in order to communicate as fully as possible with the audience.

WRITING EXERCISE ONE: LAUNDRY BASKET

1. Pretend you have to hang a basket of laundry on the line and it is a meditative experience for you, a grounding experience, as you have just received a piece of very bad news.
2. Now do it again, this time as though you are late for work and need to get the laundry on the line as quickly as possible and get out of there.
3. Now do it again, in any moved way you like, while reciting the poem 'Mary had a Little Lamb' or a prayer like the 'Hail Mary'.
4. Notice how the speaking alters the moving.
5. Now try it with some improvised words of your own.

(WRITING FOR) SILENT BODIES/EMBODIMENTS

Certainly in the academy there is a kind of tyranny of the word (Conquergood, 2002). Whether you are making art or writing a thesis, words are considered the primary 'legitimate' form of communicating new knowledge. Yet practice-led researchers (and arts-based researchers) know this is not true (Harris & Sinclair, 2014). Sure, sometimes, in order to work within the structures of the academy, we must become interlocutors, translators between performance and other practice-led work and scholarly words that can make these practices intelligible to other academics. As Vines has noted, in postgraduate dance education students are required to present "…performance work accompanied by a written minor thesis. A minor thesis typically describes, documents and articulates the philosophy of the student's artwork. This structure assumes that dancing and writing function together to form a whole" (Vines, 2010, p. 99 in Barrett & Bolt). But what if the work itself formed its own whole, a whole that was intelligible within scholarly contexts? What if moving and performing bodies could represent their own knowledge and view of reality in and of themselves?

WRITING EXERCISE TWO: SILENT SHOUT

1. Pretend you are a grateful zombie who has just become reanimated. Communicate with no words.

2. Now flirt with the person sitting across a restaurant. You are pretending to listen to your dinner companion while trying to gain the attention of the person in question.
3. Now improvise that you have just had a massive stroke and the only thing that moves is your face, especially your eyes. You cannot speak but you can use your face muscles. Tell your audience a story.
4. Write a silent 'monologue' for a still and silent body.

The best performances, both written and embodied, move beyond words on a page or a body in space and time. Peter Handke's *The Hour When We Knew Nothing of One Another* (a full-length play with no spoken words, only movements and gestures), still explores a performative 'language' of the body. When the actors assembled by the National Theatre in the UK sat down to begin work on a performance of *The Hour*, they were, at first, stumped by the proposition of "reading through" a play with no words (National Theatre Education, n.d., p. 2). Soon, though, they devised a way of coming to know the play by moving their bodies in space (for example, walking away or waking towards an event or action that's just occurred) (National Theatre Education, p. 4).

Rehearsing a play like *The Hour* asks writers and performers to pay attention to something more dynamic than words on the page, something closer to "the silent space of felt knowledge that lay beyond words and the meaning of the word 'alphabet'" (Iggulden, 2010, p. 77). We are trying to suggest that for the writer of performance, both spoken and silent, embodied and empty must equally play a role. For Annette Iggulden and others who note the embodied act of writing, there is a beautiful and necessary dance of likeness and difference, and this tension is what ultimately makes effective performance—both in the making and in the viewing (public sharing):

> The materials, colours and my act of writing created an embodied pictorial field, as much of the sense as of the mind and spirit. The alphabet, as a visual and verbal system, was developed over the centuries so that we might communicate thoughts and feelings. The medieval scribal-artist revealed the visual co-dependency of the 'positive' letters of the alphabet to their 'negative' spaces. Without this co-dependency, neither the letters nor the spaces that bound them could exist. The structure of language would collapse into glossolalia and meaninglessness without the support of silence: the evidence of its co-dependency with utterance. (Iggulden, 2010, p. 77)

Most of all, we must be willing to let our writing point equally to speaking and to performing of silences.

(WRITING FOR) VIRTUAL EMBODIMENTS

When we speak of 'virtual' and 'virtual bodies', we most often mean those existing within online worlds or digital technology (Broadhurst & Machon, 2012). But there are potent other virtual embodiments, and always have been. Sometimes, those virtual spaces are 'social imaginaries' (where imagination isn't simple thought or fantasy, but is instead as a socially organized set of practices; see Appadurai, 1996, p. 31), and sometimes they are symbolic spaces and ways of being that are etched in a collective unconscious (Jung, 1981), like a fear of the deep blue ocean, or vast 'empty' deserts, or a cultural subconscious love of the 'open road'.

Liveness and its supposed opposite represent an old but persistent binary. The long-running debate about the ontological status or nature of 'liveness' is typified by a famous contra between Philip Auslander and Peggy Phelan in which Phelan argued that performance is defined by its non-reproducible and ephemeral nature (it can only happen in the 'now', otherwise it becomes a memory and/or a representation), to which Auslander famously countered that liveness has no superiority over "…mediated recordings of all kinds in resisting commodification and capitalist appropriation" (qtd. in Roach, 2007, p. 522) and sees "ever-more permeable boundaries between the live and the mediated (as witnessed in such phenomena as lip-syncing, for instance)" (Roach, 2007, p. 522). Auslander argues that if there ever really *were* clear distinctions between live and mediatized performance, they are fading. The binary of online/offline performance raises "the question of whether there really are clear-cut ontological distinctions between live forms and mediatized ones' and in which "the opposite of the live is not the dead, but the mediatized…" (Roach, 2007, p. 522).

For some performance-makers in contemporary DIY and protest cultures, the notion of virtual publics (Laurel, 2013) holds both political power and aesthetic possibilities. In her book *Notes Toward a Performative Theory of Assembly* (2015), Judith Butler examines some of the complex dynamics of public assembly as inextricable from neoliberal and capitalist conditions. Butler views assemblies—'concerted actions of the body'—as a form of performative action (that is, to assemble is to 'say' something; the act of gathering counts as 'speech'). Gathering together (in both online and offline spaces) makes bodies (especially bodies that suffer under poverty and the abuses of prison and other oppressions) both seen *and* heard. For example, the *#BlackLivesMatter* movement is one that gained momentum in both online and offline spaces and assemblies, and relied on both for raising awareness and creating solidarity through performances of resistance, including text-based performances. Further, the visceral and affective heat of assemblies of physical bodies also goes far beyond what is said, or how. Thus, Butler's analysis of contemporary protest assemblies (like Occupy) bear parallels to performance making and writing. While Butler's body of work has continued to ask who matters as well as what bodies can be seen and valued in social spaces, performance itself (whether public political performances or theatrical ones) offers valuable enactments of bodies and lives that matter. Whether those bodies and their stories gather online or offline, the performative (inherently collective) impulse brings focus to aspects of human experience that increasingly can be overlooked in everyday social contexts.

WRITING EXERCISE THREE: IMPROVISING MARRIAGE

1. Improvise a marriage proposal to someone in front of you.
2. Now improvise a marriage proposal to someone online.
3. Now improvise a marriage proposal in the middle of an Occupy Wall Street gathering in which everything you say will be repeated out to the crowd via the 'human mic' (Note: the human microphone also known as the people's microphone is a particular form of group communication in absence of mediatized amplification of the voice. In this form, the speaker speaks in short phrases which are then repeated back by the crowd, amplifying the words to the outer reaches of the group, but also creating an embodied, interactive experience with aesthetic but also politic impact).

EXEMPLAR ONE: LOST BODIES

Here we draw on an exemplar from a play called *Surviving Jonah Salt,* which was co-written by Anne, Katharine Ash, Stephen Carlton, and Gail Evans. We use it here to show an example of bodies in space—not (as you might imagine) an innovative use of space in which to PERFORM a play, but rather it used space as a provocation/devising element in the creation of the work (in two distinct ways).

The play was written in response to Stephen's provocation that the 'outback' is a potent image in the Australian social imaginary, one that 'haunts' the (Australian) national identity in both adventurous but also fear-filled ways. Stephen contacted three other playwrights around the country and asked if we wanted to collaborate on a co-written play based around the theme and scene of the 'far North Australian outback.' We gathered only once physically in order to brainstorm the central themes and images of the play, and then again as part of the rehearsal process when the play was mounted in its first full production.

During that first meeting, after brainstorming some general themes and the central motif of 'agoraphobia as a cultural contagion', we each created a character. Mine was Jonah Salt, a 19-year-old white male suffering from some anger problems and a lack of direction. By the end of our initial in-person brainstorm, we decided as a group that Jonah would be the pivot character, and the other three characters—all women—would be related in some way to Jonah. We returned to our homes (me to Alice Springs, Gail to Darwin, Stephen to Brisbane and Katharine to northern Queensland). We wrote the rest of the script remotely, by phone or email (this was before the days of social media and Skype), creating scenes and monologues in different configurations. These scenes then began to suggest a structure for the play, and ultimately a main narrative in which Jonah inhabited both the play and the vast Australian outback with a series of ghosts, presences, and absences.

Surviving Jonah Salt is one example of how space as a conceptual provocation (writing 'into' a specific space, like a desert or a vast 'unsettled' landscape; for more on spaces in performance, see Chapter Five) can be generative in a creative collaboration, but also how space between bodies (the distance between us as collaborators) can affect not only the development of a play but its structure and content as well. This early-in-the-play monologue, which established Jonah's character, is infused with those different kinds of bodies-in-relation: between us as collaborators and also as writers all living in different regions of a 'great North' that lives so fearfully in the psyche of urban Australians.

    [JONAH, 16, white, bloodied, stands in the bush.]

Jonah: Hey! Motha-FUCKas!!!!!!!!!!!!!!!!!!! Come baaaaaaaack! You FUCKS!

    [Nothing. A car drives away into the horizon. More nothing.]

I knew this would happen.
I *told* her. I said:
Ma, you wanna go bang some guy from Tennant, go fer it. Knock yourself out. Literally. I could care less. But I don't

43

wanna go. I got my mates, I got my piece a shit KFC job, I got my CAR that's gonna be ready in a coupla weeks, but *no*. She wouldn't leave me. …

[Jonah sits and lights his LAST ciggie. He drags deeply.]

I'm gonna say something. I'm gonna be like, *Ma, I'm gone. Nah. I'm just goin. Don't give a shit where. Not stayin here, nah. Piss off. You find your own broken hearts, I find mine. That's what being grown up is, ain't it? Broken hearts and run-down roadhouses. That's what you taught me, sweetheart. Just a long line a dilapidated sheds on a deserted track. Story a ur life. Not mine.*
Shit.
I can't say that.
She'd kick my ass.

[Hears a car.]

Oh shit! Is that a car?

[Hides, scared!]

Here they come. I'll kick their freaking ASSES.
All of em.
Nobody does that to Jonah Salt and gets away with it.
15 kilometers out in the middle of nowhere! Come on,
Bring it on.

[He waits. No car appears, but he continues to scan the horizon.]

Nothing is ok from the colour of the sky to the colour of this dirt, from the deserted highway to my mother fucking some dirtbag, to me not being able to get laid no matter what I do. What's wrong with me? I'm not such a bad guy. Jesus. You'd think I have the munga or something, the way girls run from me.

[Inhales, exhales. Rest.]

I'm cool.

In this excerpt, Anne draws from a conversation between Patricia and Trish in which bodies become suspect characters in this ghostly, seemingly-empty landscape, and the audience is unsure (like the characters they are watching) whether to trust these 'bodies' or not. For a play like *Jonah Salt* (as in Ibsen's play, *Ghosts*) the real 'ghosts' are not the bodies of the dead people who haunt the living. These ghosts are more the biases and pervasive social norms that haunt and destroy those who inhabit these worlds. In *Surviving Jonah Salt,* the ghosts include the marginalisation and vilification of sex workers, fear of the 'other', the 'wild' and the untamed in white Western society, and stereotypes of (violent) young men as contagion. The bodies in *Jonah Salt* move around a central grief though too: that of the loss of the mother or the maternally intimate body, which here is enacted through the intimacy of bodies lost in the 'outback', a vast landscape of non-intimacy. Unlike Ibsen's *Ghosts*, the characters in *Jonah Salt* yearn for that lost intimacy, act out in pursuit of it, and continue to suffer from its failed attempts.

In texts like *Jonah Salt*, spaces themselves can become/perform another kind of body. Here the outback became its own character, with a 'body' all its own. Some might argue that as a 'character' in this play it also had agency and actions of its own. Would you agree or disagree that an 'inanimate' character can have agency (for more on this see Stewart, 2007; Manning, 2013; Massumi, 2002)? In this case, the desert/outback threatened the human characters, but it also embraced them, absorbed them, and, at times, comforted them. In this way, the desert performed as a kind of body that did what these 'human' characters wished from the other human characters (but did not receive); here, nature becomes a living character with a body that is able to inter/act, as this scene excerpt shows:

Patricia	Uh-huh. Not even going to ask. Look, hon, your wig's all over the place. I happen to know a bit about emergency coiffure. You want me to fix that haystack?
	[Patricia *picks out spinifex, tucks in Trish's hair, straightens the wig, pulls out a wide-toothed comb from her bag and starts stroking it through her hair.*]
Trish	I'm trying my best. To make amends.
Patricia	Sure you are. We all are.
Trish	Really.
Patricia	You've cut your hands.
Trish	No really. I had an epiphany. I think it was. Never had one before, so it could have been just a big glitch, but it didn't feel glitchy, you know. Glitches flick, like flick through you.

Then they're gone. This was like a dump, a dump of a feeling. Without words. Just a fullness, like I suddenly ate too much. There I was, this big roly poly woman out in the desert, full as a goog, suddenly large and full of this, this, urgency and there was this boy.

[Patricia *stops what's she doing and stares at her.*]

This boy who needed my help and, and there was spinifex and I knew, I knew, yes, that was it.

Patricia	Boy?
Trish	Yes. Yes, here's this boy. Yes, I nearly ran him over. Of all the people to drive by, yes, I was it.
Patricia	You hit him?
Trish	Nearly.
Patricia	Is he alright?
Trish	Fit as a fiddle. Remarkable how they bounce back at that age.
Patricia	…Where is he?
Trish	He's out the front.
Patricia	He's what?
Trish	You heard. Come out here to see his mother.

[Patricia *drops the comb—freezes.*]

Trish	Some washed up old lush. Been around the traps, if you know what I mean. Got it fixed in his mind she's shacked up here with some bloke. Comin' up on a surprise visit –
Patricia	What's he look like?
Trish	I dunno. Sixteen. Scruffy. Smart mouth.
Patricia	That your banged up ute out the front?
Trish	Yes.
Patricia	Keep describing him to me.
Trish	Dunno. His name was Jonah. The boy. As in the fairytale about the whale. He was beaten up by his seven brothers who were jealous of him and left to die in the wilderness. Or something. Can't remember the whole story. Anyway, I was the whale, sent by God, came fishtailing to him and swallowed him whole and brought him home. Score one to Nurse Betty.
Patricia	*[Disappointed, realising she's not talking about someone new.]* Oh.

Trish   Well there's no need to sound so disappointed. I can go back and finish him off if you like.

Patricia   You know, the more I think about it, the less sense it makes. 'Jonah'. It's not right. That's not his name.

Trish   Well that was the name he gave me.

Patricia   Yeah—and apparently you're Nurse frikkin' Betty. People lie, sweetheart. Life's a puzzle. And sometimes the pieces don't quite fit.

Trish   *[Eyeing her suspiciously.]* You can say that again.

Patricia   The numbers don't quite add up. I mean, I know, technically it's not possible. If he's sixteen. He was born on the day, the same day my boy turned sixteen. But, what if—[cut to]—

…And so I never did get to make that trip. Not that year. I waited sixteen years to see your face again, and I missed you by a coupla days. But I've made this journey every year since then, Brendan. Every year, I plunge off into the darkness, from this strange, quiet limbo, and I arrive upon this godforsaken place in the desert, in the deep, deep North. And each year, it feels like I'm still living, because part of me probably is. And each year I get a little bit older, and for one day I still shit and fart and burp and breathe, and there's always people here, this odd assortment of tormented souls, and they can all see me, and I can talk to them, and so I think if I keep coming here, if I wait long enough, then maybe you'll turn up and I can talk to you, and maybe time will have stood still for you too and you'll still be sixteen years old—a rebellious kid making contact behind his parent's backs—or maybe you'll be a grown man.

Maybe.

Maybe you'll just want to stop and talk for a while.

Maybe you'll forgive me.

Maybe you'll believe me when you hear my story.

Maybe not.

But it'd be nice.

It'd be nice just to see you again. Just to have a chinwag. Have a glass of red, smoke a couple of cigarettes, and have a chinwag…

[beat]

There are places in this world that never get dark. Days up North—I mean way up North—where the sun never sets at all. True story. All of the stories, true...

[Lights fade.]

WRITING EXERCISE FOUR: MAKING PEOPLE WITH WORDS

This exercise is drawn from Young Playwrights' Inc.'s, 'Writing on Your Feet' curriculum. The exercise is called 'The Need to Tell':

1. Complete the character questionnaire below for TWO characters (be as specific as you can):
   - What is this character's name?
   - Who is this person (How old are they? What does they do for a living? Do they have a family?)
   - What is special or unique about this character (concentrate on things that can be observed: How does this person talk? Walk? Dress? Behave?)
   - Where is his or her favourite place in the world? (For example: A restaurant. What kind of restaurant? Expensive or cheap? Do they eat there all the time or is it the first time? What is the name of the restaurant?)
   - How do they feel about being there? Are they happy? Are they sad? Are they angry? Are they worried? Why?
   - What does this character dream about? Need? Want? What is stopping them from getting these things?
2. For each character, give them 1) a secret they have never told ANYONE, and 2) a fact that they have a *need to tell*. The principle of this exercise is that everyone has a need to tell something, and that this need drives most of the action of our lives. There may be more than one 'thing' that they need to tell, but you decide for your character what their need is this time.
3. Use one character's need to tell to establish the place of the scene. For example, if young Jack's need to tell is that he wants to find his birthmother, then make the scene happen at a conference for birthmothers.
4. Let two actors play the two characters, at the agreed scene. The scene is going to be improvised. The actors continue to pursue their 'want' through expressing their 'need to tell' fact as often as necessary, and by hiding their 'secret' but letting it continue to drive their actions. So each character has two motivations: one is spoken, one is hidden. When the 'heat' or momentum seems to go out of the improvisation, you (as writer/director/

deviser) can make up another secret that compromises and motivates one of the characters. If, in our Jack example, he wants to find his birthmother but is scared also to find his birthmother because he was born female, this will alter and drive his actions in this improvisation.

5. At any point, stop the actors and write. You can either audio/video record the improvisation to that point and then write the 'rest' of the scene as you imagine it, or you can transcribe what you have heard/seen in the scene so far.

EXEMPLAR TWO: SMELLY BODIES

I rather like the smell of absurdity in the morning. (Robbins, 2001, p. 151)

Bodies smell, and olfactory impact is one of the most powerful intersubjective and affective triggers around. Theatre practitioners have long recognised the potential of this most evocative sensory stimulator, and worked in different ways to critically and practically incorporate it into the sensory experience of theatre and performance (Auslander, 1999; Di Benedetto, 2011; Collins & Nisbet, 2010; Bradley, 2014; Laurel, 2013; Brook, 1996; Grotowski, 2012; Schechner, 2007; Shepherd-Barr, 1999; Banes & Lepecki, 2012; Vroon, 1997). Stephen De Benedetto offers a useful history of the considerable theatrical experimentation with olfaction in the 20th century. He says, "the use of smell communicates to us in an intimate way" (Di Benedetto, 2011, p. 158) and indeed one of the unique aspects of smell as a performative communicator is not only its cultural situatedness, but its powerful stimulus to memory. In working with seniors and memory, Jane Luton (2015) details the range and intensity of memories evoked by recalling

the smells generated by a discussion as the residents recounted the carbolic smell of hospitals, the smell of the salty sea, the smell of the bush, Johnson's baby powder, the smell of a dog, of fresh-cut grass, camphor, the smell of newly baked Hokey Pokey, sulphur phosphate from the factory in Penrose, a fruitcake with brandy, and one particularly pungent smell came from memories of a children's home. (p. 145)

But while smell is certainly liked to individual memory, it is also most certainly culturally-situated and constructed. Like theatre, smell is inextricable from the acculumations and assemblages of not only cultural groups but historical moments:

Historically, the cultural uses of aromas in the West diminished with the hygiene campaigns of the late 19th and early 20th centuries, since the spread of disease was linked to foul odors. Perhaps the deodorization of the theatre was in some ways connected to the scientific ambitions of naturalism, to an idea of the theatre as a sanitized laboratory… The deoderization of the modern theatre may also be one facet of a conscious move away from—even an antagonism toward—religious ritual. (Banes, 2010, p. 348)

Stacy attended the famed and intimate performance piece *On the Scent* performed by Leslie Hill, Helen Paris, and Lois Weaver, in the New York apartment of theatre scholar Marvin Carlson. These authors describe "arriving in Marvin Carlson's midtown apartment in New York City in 2004. Helen is lying in the bed, a beautiful antique wooden bed, the bed Marvin Carlson was born in. Leslie is in the narrow galley kitchen the Carlsons' describe as 'perfect for reheating Chinese takeout'. Bookshelves line the sitting-room walls, like a library. Lois Weaver has left a small lipstick kiss on the white wall" (Hill & Paris, 2014, p. 44). The intimacy of these performances, which initially were performed for only one or two audience members at a time (later up to four) have been widely documented, but Stacy recalls the intensity of attending the performance as the second audience member to/with performance scholar Peggy Phelan in a river of adjectives:

…the sultry heat of the August early evening, waiting on the sidewalk, nervous sweat running down my back, for Peggy Phelan (THE Peggy Phelan) to arrive. Then, key thrown down from a second story window, the creek of the ancient elevator and awkward silence of our ascent, entering the cloud of your mother's stale perfume swirling—somehow—around Lois Weaver (THE Lois Weaver), who is seated on the living room sofa. The sharp smell of popcorn and cayenne and charred meat Leslie (yes, THE LESLIE HILL) cooks in the kitchen and the cloud of smoke that rises like the terrifying photographs of the atom bomb when she pushes the skillet under the running tap, the clean and sweet smell of the whiskey that (THE) Helen Paris paints on her lips as she tosses and turns in the bed with such jumpy, magnetic power it makes even (THE) Peggy Phelan giggle a bit nervously…

Such intimacies were not limited to but enhanced by its olfactory focus, one described here by two of the show's co-performers:

On the Scent (2003) is a performance about the relationship between the sense of smell, emotion and memory...You are given an address and a time of arrival, 3.30pm. You make your way to the place: an apartment building in Shanghai; a detached house in a leafy street in Cambridge; a gothic mansion in Porto Alegre. It is raining. You are the last to arrive. Three strangers stand at the front door. You are handed a key. You hesitate, look to the others for confirmation, they shrug, then nod. You turn the key and enter the house. You smell the strangeness of another person's home... (Hill & Paris, 2014, p. 25)

Hill and Paris' text talks in depth about olfactory performance, in particular about *On the Scent*. They note, "Smell can be a hugely potent player in live performance, a pervasive, silent stalker that seeps inside us, unlocking past memories, secrets, feelings and intensities. Both live performance and the olfactory share an intangibility, an ungraspability that is a defining part of the very nature of each" (Hill & Paris, 2014, p. 40). In many ways, smell is the most *affective* (the experience of an intensity that is pre-conscious and unnamable) of the senses, and for this reason we believe that smell does play a role in theatre, even when it is an implied smell, like for example the smell of toast being invoked by a performance with an untoasted piece of bread.

Rachel Fensham (2009) examines how 'smell-bodies' carry audiences the untamed, messy and unwanted places we crave to return to and to embrace. "Through the corporeality of the actor's body, the smell-bodies enable the leaky, messiness of the text to mix with the social but they also reveal the practices that make the symbolic repress figures that disturb the social order" (p. 172). In considering Barry Kosky's Australian production of *King Lear*, Fensham theorises play as an assemblage of masculinities, creating a kind of language-lessness that results in 'smell-bodies' of masculine experience and intersubjectivity.

As we have noted, throughout the 20th century "various artists (both mainstream and avant-garde) repeatedly attempted to renew the sense of smell as part of the theatrical experience...using aroma both to challenge and to expand the realist aesthetic. In the 1990s, olfactory effects in performance became particularly pronounced" (Banes, 2010, p. 349), and the documentation of its affective power did too. Smell is, ultimately and like live performance itself, beautifully ephemeral. "...Smell, like taste, is a sensation of the moment, it cannot be preserved. We do not know what the past smelled like, and in the future our own odor will be lost" (Classen, Howes, & Synnott, 1995, p. 204). If it's true that "sight and hearing are, classically, *senses at a distance,* as opposed to the immediacy not only of touch but of taste and smell" (Blau, 2010, p. 53), we propose that writing as well as performing smell can bring all your audiences' senses closer. Try this writing exercise to flex your smelly muscles:

WRITING EXERCISE FIVE: SMELL IT LIKE IT IS

We all know that smell is the most evocative sense of the (at least) five we have, and the last to go. But how do you evoke the smells of a place for an audience who may never have been there in person? Writing for performance is a bodily act, and always implies within it a bodily sensation, experience, and materiality. So how might you make smells with words?

1. Go outside and pick something green. If there is nothing green in your environment that you can reach within walking distance, you are in trouble. No, seriously, just write about that. But if there is, pick it and walk back to your writing place, close your eyes, crush it between your fingers, smell it and write. Not what does it smell LIKE, but what does it evoke? Does mint smell 'fresh', or does it smell like a summer afternoon at 3 o'clock in South Carolina on your grandma's porch? Does it smell 'green', or does it smell like freedom or rage or love? Write what you smell.
2. Now go into the farthest back corner of the darkest dirtiest closet in the place where you are. Sit there or grab something from in there, smell it with your eyes closed, and start writing. Does this contrast with the outdoor smell you just wrote, or does it complement it?
3. Now find a non-stationary living thing (recognising that plants too are alive): a dog, a fish, a kid, your partner, your parent, a gerbil, whatever. Look at it. Watch it. But before you smell it, sit down and write for a while. What does the visual of it evoke in you? Can you recall other encounters with that being, or one like it? Does seeing a dog remind you of a pee smell, when you were a kid and your puppy peed on your clothes? Does seeing a gerbil or hamster remind you of the small rib of celery or something else you used to feed it? I know when I see pictures of my dog Luna (now deceased) I always smell the soft baby smell of the top of her head. She never smelled doggy, always like a baby. Hint: the evocation of smells in writing is often linked to other fluids and functions that link smell to other senses: the smell of shit often calls up the fear of being sick; the smell of rotten food calls up the anxiety of poverty. Think about the ways in which smell evokes other sensory or emotive responses. One way into this, if you are having difficulty, is to ask yourself the question 'Who smells?'—as in, 'Who smells this smell?'

4. Lastly, find a way to go to the alley behind the busiest restaurant in your town/city/village. Usually there are bins back there, and usually they are overflowing. If you're lucky, it's nearly garbage day and the bins and alleyway are festering. Hard as it may be, stand in the alley and breathe deeply through your nose.
5. Write about what it feels like to be assaulted by a smell.

EXEMPLAR THREE: *365 DAYS/365 PLAYS* BY SUZAN-LORI PARKS

Erin Manning has extended our wonderings about bodies, embodiments, and what it means to be alive as and through making—in particular, through dance. Our bodies continuously interact with other bodies, and perform relationships that change us and push us collectively forward. She does not write about bodies as 'things', but as 'doings', and reminds us that we are organic blobs always in motion, always perfectly where we are now, but still never quite arriving:

> Vitality forms 'are the most fundamental of all felt experience.' They are inherent in each coming-to-act, bringing forth a speciation that always exceeds containment (Stern, 2010, p. 8). These speciations occur in the between of experience and experiencing where embodiment is not-yet. They meet as tendencies, as proclivities. Arm meets rosebush to become gardening-tendency, thorn meets sound to become weapon, disintegrating rock meets water to become raft. Bodies, life-forms do emerge, but never as fully formed, never 'as such': something always escapes the delineation of the coming-to-act, and something always exceeds it. The body, the individual, life as such is but a shorthand for a million speciations, organic and inorganic, intertwining. (2013, p. 199)

One of our favourite playwrights is Suzan-Lori Parks, because she writes about life as it is in a way that makes it seem always becoming, and always not quite 'real' (because, why should she?). Parks' play *365 Days/365 Plays* uses the rhythms and motions of everyday life to create theatre that demonstrates Manning's ideas, proclivities, and emergence. For the writer of performance, this motion and shape-shifting is the key to dramatic tension and high stakes in the script. If you ask us, everything Suzan-Lori Parks writes is interesting because she documents the big ideas of her place and time through the heartwrenching and tender minutae of everyday life. Each of her works is interesting for a different reason. While she has strong themes that run through all her plays, she is one of the most inventive writers on the American stage today. In her opening to the published version of *365 Days/365 Plays* plays, Parks says:

> I got this notion to write a play a day for a whole year… 'Yeah baby, that'd be cool,' Paul said. And so I started writing. It was November 13, 2002. I thought about waiting until January 1 to begin, but I wanted to keep it real, so I started right where I was, working with whatever I had at the moment. So that day I began writing a series of plays called *365 Days/365 Plays*. Every day for the next year I would wake up and ask myself, "Ok, so what's the play?" and I wrote what came. The plan was that no matter what I did, how busy I was, what other commitments I had, I would write a play a day, every single day, for a year. It would be about being present and being committed to the artistic process every single day, regardless of the 'weather.' It became a daily meditation, a daily prayer celebrating the rich and strange process of a writing life. (Parks, 2006, n.p)

This meditation of Parks' became an interactive and inter/national theatrical sensation called *The 365 National Festival*, involving thousands of theatre folks and hundreds of theatres across the United States, which presented all 365 plays and lasted an entire year. Now we are not all writers of the calibre of Suzan-Lori, but we can all use our writing practice as a rhythm to our lives, a meditation on where we are now. So:

WRITING EXERCISE SIX: A PLAY A DAY

1. Wake up.
2. Write today's play.
3. Do it again tomorrow.

BODIES AND…

In this chapter, we have explored how bodies carry the performance word—that is, how words are embodied by performer and, in turn, are joined with the bodies of the audience (through sight, sound, smell, and touch). Bodies speak and move, shout and are silent, and perform in both in-person and virtual spaces. Bodies make the words of a performance text come alive. But there's another sense in which text is also a living and lively force with a will of its own. In Chapter Four, we consider the 'thingness' of text as another kind of embodiment in words.

THINGS

MAKING THINGS MEAN

As we have noted throughout this book, writing is a symbolic, representational practice. We make sense of things by assigning meaning to signs—words, sounds, images, and objects—through a process of representation. Cultural studies theorist Stuart Hall (1997) writes that representation is a process of assigning meaning to language and culture that happens in two moves. The first move in the process is to give meaning to the world by calling it up a concept in our minds and then connecting that mental representation with specific people, events, or objects in the world. For example, saying 'dog' or 'birthday' or 'bicycle' first calls up a mental picture of that person or animal, event, or thing. The second move in the process is to create a sign that refers to that mental picture through a shared system of meaning (words, symbols, sounds, images, and objects). What Hall calls 'systems of representation' are processes and practices that produce shared meaning. And so performance is a system of representation that makes things mean and meaningful for an audience.

Ways of making things mean vary, of course. The representational view, which connects a mental representation to an external 'thing' in the world, assumes we have reliable and accurate access to signs through a clear process of representation. However, other views hold that signs do not simply connect a mental picture with an identifiable external reality. While signs *carry* meaning, the relationship between a sign and a concept or referent is arbitrary and shifts over time. For example, if we say the sign 'dog,' what referent comes to your mind? The picture that comes to mind for Anne is a black Cocker Spaniel who smells like a baby. The picture that comes to mind for Stacy is a white Havanese about the size of a meatloaf who likes to eat broccoli. This example illustrates how representations do not simply depict a reality or show us 'the way things are' because the mental picture of 'dog' that you came up with when you read the third sentence of this paragraph was probably NOT a black Cocker Spaniel who smells like a baby OR a white Havanese who likes to eat broccoli but some OTHER dog altogether.

In another example, the sign 'dog' might not refer to an animal with four legs and a tail, but instead to a politician you find contemptible, a bad investment, or an unattractive person or object. Or further, the 'dog' might refer to a person, event, or object that has no shared association with the SIGN dog, but instead with another referent—perhaps a grandmother or a bicycle.

Using language and symbols—including writing for performance—is a social process of interpretation through which culture and the 'real' is determined and also questioned. Because of this, we can write (and read or audience) culture as a collection of 'signs'—language through which that culture is communicated and challenged. This practice of reading signs is referred to as 'semiotics'. In a semiotic approach, persons, events, and things can be written and read as 'texts'. We can also say that 'texts' can be written as persons and events, as discussed in Chapter Two, and also as objects or things. Considering writing for performance as writing *things* asks us to differently attend to the relationship between our selves (subjects) and the texts we create (things). Rather than viewing texts as a personal comment on the 'the way things are' in an external world 'out there', the texts we create are instead animated and alive—they move and do things in the world in their own way and of their own accord. Here, texts are things with lives and wills of their own, in relation to and separate from their human counterparts. Or as anthropologist Michael Taussig puts it, "words can be links to viscerality, into the thingness of things" (2006, p. x). In this view, the 'thingness' of texts means that they can show us how things do or don't make sense in ways that don't neatly line up with ideas about the well-made play, plot and character, and depicting a world to an audience. Instead, the thingness of texts insists that writing for performance is a way of questioning and constructing an(other) view of the world.

MAKING THINGS MEAN DIFFERENTLY

But where did this way of thinking about and writing performance come from? As we noted in Chapter One, writing for performance follows an historical trajectory that parallels the development of modern society, from the ancient Greeks through to contemporary performance artists. Performance makers are often part of an avant-garde—experimenters and innovators who are at the forefront of social, political and aesthetic movements. In the wake of World War I (1914–18) and again after World War II (1939–1945), avant-garde writers and other artists questioned the modern logic of progress and capitalism. They asked how the arts could go on telling the same kinds of stories in the same kinds of ways when the world had witnessed the cultural, social, and economic devastations of war and the genocide of the Holocaust. In response, artists of all kinds—writers, dancers, visual artists, musicians, and theatre and performance makers—sought new forms of writing that rejected traditional conventions of storytelling in favor of those in which texts become things with a sense and logic of their own. For example, the Dadaists created texts and objects that defied typical modes of storytelling and meaning making. Designed as critique of modern culture and an attack on logic and rational thought, the Dadaists created texts (most often poems) by beginning with a source such as a newspaper or magazine article, well-known work of fiction, encyclopedia article, police report, etc., and using techniques including chance operations (throwing darts, throwing dice, the ancient Chinese divination method the *I-Ching*) to create new texts independent of the author's intention or design. Tristan Tzara (1920) a key figure in the Dada movement, offers these instructions on how 'To Make a Dadaist Poem':

Take a newspaper.
Take some scissors.
Choose from this paper an article the length you want to make your poem.
Cut out the article,
Next carefully cut out each of the words that make up this article and put them all in a bag.
Shake gently,
Next take out each cutting one another the other.
Copy conscientiously in the order in which they left the bag.
The poem will resemble you.
And there you are—an infinitely original author of charming sensibility, even though unappreciated by the vulgar herd. (n.p.)

While this technique is not without humor, it is also meant as a critique of the certainty of modern culture. Dada poems are designed to shock their readers so they might see the familiar and everyday—what's reported in a newspaper or magazine—in new and startling ways (Rubin, 1968, p. 42; see also Brecht's *verfremdungseffekt*, or *v-effect* described in Jameson, 1998). In other words, the Dadaists and other avant-garde movements created art that helped readers and audience members see things differently.

GLUING THINGS TOGETHER: COLLAGE TECHNIQUES

Tzara's how 'To Make a Dadist Poem' asks us to pay attention to how we make the raw material of language mean *differently* through the practice of collage. Collage, from the French *coller*, or 'to glue,' is the process of creating performance works by combining source materials from one context—words, images, three-dimensional objects, bodies, sounds, projections, etc.—and placing them into another (Larbalestier, 1990, p. 7; see also Brockelman, 2001). Each element in a collage has a dual function—it (1) refers to an external reality and (2) it re-imagines or (under)cuts the meanings we have previously assigned to that reality (Perloff, 1983, p. 10). Collage makes the familiar seem strange and as a result, it puts "everything into question" (Kilgard, 2009, p. 3).

Amy Kilgard is a performer and writer who uses collage techniques, which she says opens us up to the "possibilities (perhaps miraculous) of the meaning-making process" (2009, p. 2). Her solo performance, *Triskaidekaphobia: 13 Consumer Tragedies*, introduces us to thirteen different characters are caught up in an endless cycle of consumerism, including a cashier who becomes consumed by a big box store and a compulsive collector who endlessly reconciles his obsessions. Kilgard collages together her and others' experiences of consumer encounters, juxtaposing experiences of consumer desire with the work of theft prevention and the hype of holiday shopping.

Collage techniques include doubleness, juxtaposition, and repetition. *Doubleness* points to the liveness and 'thingness' of the elements of the performance, including texts, but also characters, movements, and objects and suggests how these elements have lives outside of the performance as well. For example, in *Triskaidekaphobia*, a shopping bag from the Smithsonian Institution Air and Space Museum that she acquired on a family vacation when she was seven suggests other, previous uses outside of and before/after the performance. The shopping bag reminds us that each element in the performance has ties to the world and a history that expands beyond it.

EXEMPLAR ONE: *TRISKAIDEKAPHOBIA* BY AMY KILGARD

The Tragedy of Desire

I'm looking for the perfect bag. Maybe you've seen it. Maybe you have it. Maybe you'll give it to me? You see I'm an archivist of consumerism. A phenomenologist of neoliberal happenings.

Or, a person who just wants to understand performances of desire.

You see I'm restarting my collection—the one collection I had as a child—my bag collection. Don't look at me like that. I came by this naturally. Ok. Ok. I'll show you.

This is my diary. See, it has a lock and a key. I like to write in it every Friday—when I get my allowance.

Allowance 25 cents. That means I have 16 quarters, 17 dimes, 22 nickels, and 53 pennies: Total $7.33.

I'm not kidding. And I got it from both sides of my family. My father's father, my granddad, never bought anything on credit. He would walk into the Chrysler dealership cash in hand. And my mother's parents had a big jar of dimes on the dresser in their bedroom. They never spent a dime!

It makes sense that I turned to bags as a collection. Bags are free. Bags are extra. People don't see the value in bags. And so, sometimes they give them to you.

Look, I know you have some bags out there. I mean, San Francisco is filled with interesting one-of-a-kind places that have great one-of-a-kind bags. And I know the bag ordinance means they're not free anymore. And I'm all in favor of the ordinance. But, do you know how much they cost now? They cost ten cents. They cost dimes. And I have my own jar of dimes.

The first bag in my collection was a crisp, white, square paper bag from the Smithsonian Institution Air and Space Museum that I got on a family vacation when I was seven and my brother was five. I kept it because it reminded me that we had been there—the museum and outer space. My brother grew up to be an astronomer. And I grew up to have a bag collection—from places I had been and from those I had yet to see.

OK. Now that they're all laid out, I'm going to show you a few of the most interesting bags and then we can reorganize them, if you want to. Oh, look. This one is from Six Flags. It's a really old one. I got this one at least seven years ago. I was a really little kid. As you can see, it has a roller coaster on it, which makes it fun. It's pretty small and it doesn't have handles and it's kind of flimsy, so it's not really useful. It's made of plastic which means it won't decompose as quickly, which is a plus and a minus, I suppose.

OK. Now, this one I just got from my friend Lisa Kay. Her family went to Austria last year and she brought me this bag from Mozart's birthplace museum. See, that's Mozart's music on there. And feel this, it's made of that really nice, expensive, paper. Listen. That's the sound of good paper.

OK. I know this one isn't all that amazing to look at. But every time I see it, I remember visiting Cafe Du Monde, in New Orleans. Beignets? Yum. It is sturdy, and it has good handles, and it does have its name on it. So, that's something.

Oh, but this is my favorite! Just look at it. (Pause, as if waiting for them to say what it is.) It's the Grand Canyon. Printed on a bag. I think it's the most beautiful bag in the collection. Don't you? …

A couple of years ago, I went to a professional conference in New Orleans and I went to Cafe Du Monde and had beignets. Yum. And when I got back to San Francisco, someone had left me a Cafe Du Monde bag in my mailbox at school. Don't you see what that means. One of the bags from my original collection found its way back to me. The bag fairy brought me a Cafe du Monde bag so that I would re-start my collection. Now I've started getting a little bit excited about bags again. Now, I know that the last time you went on vacation, you went someplace cool. And you didn't bring me those bags. I'm just saying. (n.d., pp. 1–4)

Juxtaposition asks us to pay attention to the relationships between elements in the collage, including texts, characters, sounds, and images by putting deliberately different and disparate things next to each other. In *Triskaidekaphobia*, Kilgard juxtaposes narratives about consumption, layering stories about collecting—clothes, ipods, makeup, music, jewelry, DVDs—one upon the other. Juxtaposition doesn't provide the 'connections' between these disparate things, but instead relies on readers and audiences to make their own connections. As part of this collage of collected things, Kilgard offers a narrative that begins by considering the definition of the word collection that leads to an ever-expanding consideration of the insatiable desire to collect:

The Tragedy of the Partial

Collection: a whole greater than the sum of its parts—a cliché that itself is greater than the sum of its previous clichéd uses because the collection, the set, the group, is the idea that spawned that particular cliché in the first place—so you and I might find ourselves partial to it.
  click–click–click–click–click–click–click
Partial: A word with many definitions, a fractured word, a word with senses that fan out in different directions—a positive adjective meaning

favoring, a negative adjective marking a *lack*, a musical term naming any one of the ascending overtones that combine to make a single audible tone. Seven harmonic partials, like seven tiny figures, are part of any tone in the Western octave system. Seven partials give each tone its own unique halo of higher overtones, 'upper partials' that fan out into an infinity of higher and higher frequencies...

   click–click–click–click–click–click–click

A firm, stable collection of consumer products, one without lack, one that has all its parts in careful order: that's what I favor. You? Do you, too, see the absence on your bookshelf, the bookshelf that holds an author's sixth book and her eighth? Do you, too, create a new need every time you fill one at the store? When your passion for film history—reading books about old Hollywood, collecting DVDs of Scorsese and Coppola films, and so on—leads you, too, to Hitchcock, do Hitchcock DVDs become for you, in time, not simply a possible addition but a necessary one, an unavoidable one? Do you, too, feel that without them, your grasp of film would have a huge gap, a lack? ...

   click–click–click–click–click–click–click

In the span of just a few months, since just this past fall, have your shelves, too, somehow gone from featuring no Hitchcock titles of any kind to featuring 31 DVD cases encompassing all but four of his available films; two boxed sets of seasons of the TV series; and nine books? Is this really the only way you can understand *Psycho*?

   click–click–click–click–click–click–click

Anytime *you* go anywhere within eyeballing distance of Rasputin Records, do *you* strain to keep in mind that you don't have space in your house for this kind of obsessive collecting? That you don't have money, despite being middle–class, to pay for collections fanning out at this pace? That you despise, or tell yourself you despise, allowing mega–corporations like Sony to titillate you with freshly packaged media and to profit from your compulsions? Why not use the library? Why do you need to *own* all of these pieces of art that have been framed as consumable? Are you, along with me, still reaching for an answer to that?

   click–click–click–click–click–click–click

Do you, with me, suspect that this compulsive collecting will continue, nevertheless, in some form? It's become its own kind of muscle memory now, a way you get juiced that you *cannot* replace. You've cultivated a high for yourself that depends on a tightly linked set of physical behaviors and psychological responses: You step into Rasputin or whatever store you have in mind, without ever relying on any kind of physical list because these lists all live in your mind all the time, they are a part of your mind, a series of 'stops' that guide you around the store in precise rhythm—from Dylan to My Morning Jacket to Radiohead to Steely Dan to XTC, ***click–click–click–click–click–click–click*** through the stacks of long cases holding the CDs in place, looking for good prices ***click–click–click–click–click–click–click*** on the *Best of the Mono Recordings* from last year, the one with the blue cover, ***click–click–click–click–click–click–click*** there are plenty of copies of *Two Against Nature* but that damn DVD–audio release is impossible to find, ***click–click–click–click–click–click–click*** why is the *Dukes of Stratosphear* reissue not coming down in price yet, ***click–click–click–click–click–click–click*** to the DVDs, Hitchcock now a new 'permanent' stop in any media store, and 'permanent' stops only get added rarely, every year or so, Hitchcock and My Morning Jacket this year, ***click–click–click–click–click–click–click***…

You and I are stable tones at the base of the overtones of all of these infinitely fanning consumer collections that we have now and that we may someday have. We want to own them because they are like clothes, like skin. You and I only ring true to ourselves and to one another when we hear all these partials, when they live around us, all around us, a web of material safety, each one precious and beautiful. You and I may be able to change this, someday; but for now, it's an image of self that resonates; we are partial to it.

What's next? (n.d., pp. 25–28)

A third characteristic of collage in performance is *repetition*. Repetition of elements, such as texts, forms, colors, materials or textures, or sounds helps audiences pay attention to the doubled nature of the disparate fragments in a collage, as well as to create relationships and resonances among them. Repetition of the ***click–click–click–click–click–click–click*** in the narrative above repeats the sound of flipping through CD cases in the record store, the jarring rhythm of the *Psycho* soundtrack, the click click click collection coming together, part by part. Kilgard also repeats and expands the early story of her shopping bag collection by returning to it near the end of the performance, repeating the themes of desire, the image of the bags as holders of stories, one nested inside another and another, 'bags full of bags full of bags' (n.d., p. 30).

The Tragedy of Desire

I'm on my way home from my sophomore year of college and I've decided it's time to get rid of my collection. It's taking up a lot of room in my closet and Mama would really like to have some of that space. And I don't really need it anymore. The collection's gotten huge! Three suitcase-sized bags full of bags. I start laying them out, un-nesting them. They quickly cover my whole room. So I leave the room and I lay them in a path down the hall and through the family room and down the back steps into the yard and across the yard. And my parents live in South Georgia. And they have a huge live oak tree in the back of the back yard. This is one of those trees that lives in our cultural imagination of the South. I mean, it's huge, and it has Spanish moss hanging from the branches. So I lay the bags through the back yard to the base of this tree. And I turn back toward the house and I walk my path of bags. And I don't exactly tell each one goodbye, not like boo hoo, but I do spend a moment with each one, remembering when and how I got it, who gave it to me, what stories it contained, all the places I had been, and all the places I had not been, but had been in my mind. And when I reached the end of the path in my bedroom, I walked the path one more time, this time packing the bags back up. Nesting them again. One by one. Through the hallway, through the family room, down the back steps, through the yard, to the base of the tree, by the end carrying three enormous bags full of bags full of bags full of bags full of nothing. And I carried them past the tree and into the alley. And I left them with the other bags of garbage. Except for this one. I kept this one. It's not really so much a bag any more. I mean, it's really just the shell of a bag. But it is still sufficient to hold the stories. I mean, I'm looking for the perfect story. Maybe you've heard it. Maybe you know it. Maybe you have a new one. I am, you know, an archivist. (n.d., pp. 29–30)

The example of *Triskaidekaphobia* shows us how collage asks us to consider how things might mean differently. Through juxtaposing materials from multiple worlds, making doubled/multiple readings of those materials, and using repetition to emphasize the relationships among those disparate elements, we create performance texts that are open-ended and unfinished. We also create works that show us how writing for performance is a sense-making and sensory, as well as a material and meaningful experience.

WRITING EXERCISE ONE: CUT-UP AND FOLD-IN METHODS (AFTER WILLIAM S. BURROUGHS)

Writer William S. Burroughs pioneered the 'cut up method,' which he says brings to writers the collage techniques used by painters, filmmakers, and photographers. He believed that the best writing is writing that is spontaneous. And while you can't will spontanaiety, you "can introduce the unpredictable spontaneous factor with a pair of scissors" ('William S. Burroughs Cut-Ups'). One version of Burroughs's cut-up method is to:

1. Take a page of writing and cut it down the middle, both horizontally and vertically.
2. Label the sections 1, 2, 3, and 4.
3. Next, rearrange the sections so that section 4 is joined with section 1 and section 3 is joined with section 2 to form a new page.

In another version of this technique, Burroughs advises writers to take a poem written by "any poet or writer you fancy" ('William S. Burroughs Cut-Ups'). Type out several selected passages, filling the page with excerpts. Now, Burroughs advises, "Cut the page. You have a new poem. As many poems as you like" ('William S. Burroughs Cut-Ups'). Alternatively, you can use text-collaging computer programs such as the Poem Collage Generator to do the collaging for you: http://www.languageisavirus.com/poem-collage.php#.VtYXQbTi_5k. To use Burroughs's 'fold-in' technique:

1. Select a page of text—one that you've written or one written by someone else—and fold it down the middle vertically.
2. Place the folded text on another page of text, then read it across (half of one text and half of the other).
3. Alternatively, you can fold a page from early (page 1) or late (page 30) into the mille of a text (page 10) to create a flash-forward or a flash-backwards in time.

Burroughs likens this method to techniques used in film or music, where we are moved forward and backwards in time through the repetition and rearrangement of visual or musical themes. He notes that when using this method he edits, deletes, and rearranges text just as he would with other writing approaches. That said, he writes that "I have frequently had the experience of writing some pages of straight narrative texts which were then folded in with other pages and found that the fold ins were clearer and more comprehensible than the original texts…Best results are usually obtained by placing pages dealing with similar subjects in juxtaposition" ('William S. Burroughs Cut-ups').

EXEMPLAR TWO: *FOUR WORDS*

Adrian Amor is a performer, poet, visual artist and teacher who uses collage techniques in making performances that are both material and meaningful. Stacy met Adrian just after he'd returned from Afghanistan at age 19 and resumed his undergraduate studies. He enrolled in two of Stacy's performance classes—performing poetry and performing social resistance. For the poetry course, Adrian created 'Four Words' for his father, who succumbed to lung cancer when he was just 54. *Four Words* used collage techniques to combine a poem, comic book cells that were filled in as the performance progressed (creating a kind of live animated graphic novel), and a letter.

The performance began with the poem, *Four Words,* which Adrian shared with the audience in a spoken word style—standing alone on the stage (in this case, at the front of a classroom). He struggled to keep his composure and focus while reciting the poem, and struggled to make contact with the audience. When he finished, Adrian was visibly relieved.

Four Words

Those four words echoed so loudly
Suspending time to a halt—frozen
My body petrified from the information overload
Thoughts and emotions concentrated to a single drop
Pulled as gravity forced its contact
Crashing, splashing onto the linoleum surface
Shattered, scattered through the sanitized stench of the cold room
Contained by the silence that followed your sentence

What the fuck? Why? Why? Why?

You were fine just a few months before then
Impressing us youngins with some old school ball
5 decades and 4 years, you were holding strong

But, the window had passed

Silently slipping its way through your veins
It had already deployed—invaded

Situating itself on your cerebral mainframe
Gripping the thin thread that kept you with us

The days went by and turned into weeks
The weeks went by and turned into months
Time flies by when it's ticking

I'll never forget those gleaming red lights
Bouncing off the season's dressing
Fading away with your faint breath on board

We were there with you—every day
Odds against us
Fighting, praying, hoping our way through the improbable task
Until you caught drift and sailed into the tear-lit night

Most performances of poems in this setting and format would end there, though in this case, the poem what only the first element in a collage of texts. After performing the poem, Adrian turned to the whiteboard in the classroom, where the four comic cells were drawn in black outline.

Next, he filled in the detail of the story of his father's cancer—the story he'd told in one form in *Four Words*—in red. He began with a dedication, 'For You, Pa,' then drew in the basketball as it swished through the net, the spread of the cancer through his father's body, the bulbs on the Christmas tree, the exhaust of the ambulance, called on Christmas Eve, and the dwindling line marking his father's respiration during his final days in the hospital. The comic tells the same story as the poem, but in different, resonating detail.

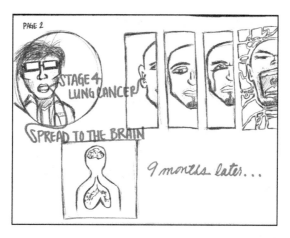

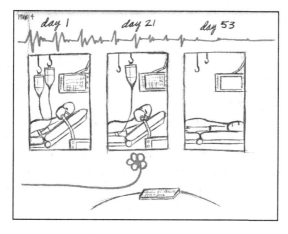

Figure 1. Four words

Adrian closed the performance with a letter, *Dear Pa*:

Dear Pa,

I want you
to know
that we are
doing okay.

We are healing.
Some days are harder than others, but
we are holding strong.
I wish you could see
me perform.
I think you would be amazed.
Pa, thank you for all that you
have done.
You have truly inspired me.

I miss you
so much.

I love you, Pa.
Life is preciously short.

Cherish it.

Laugh.
Love.
Learn.
Let go.
Live.

Adrian turned and faced the audience, holding up a sheet of paper with the words 'Dear Pa' written in large, red typescript. He didn't speak, but instead showed the letter to the audience, page, by page, each containing a few words or a photo of Adrian's father and his family. Again, the words and theme of the performance are repeated: Dear Pa, the red lights, the difficulty, the loss. Again, Adrian tried to maintain his composure, though he did not hold back his tears. Instead, he looked directly into the audience's eyes, and we repeated, shared, and repeated again the love and the letting go. He says performing the work "helped me to reflect and move on from a difficult chapter in my life" (Amor, 2016).

Taken together, the performance was part love letter, part eulogy, and part inspirational text about what we face when a loved one dies (you can see a video of the performance at: https://www.youtube.com/watch?v=tj7XRjs8qgk). He believes creating the work using collage techniques gave the audience "different perspectives [on] my thoughts and emotions. As a result, my audience understood and felt a piece of my past, emotions, and thoughts." All of the elements of the work are compelling on their own, but through the juxtaposition, double-meaning, and repetition of elements, they create a collage performance that exists not only on the page, but as a 'thing in the world' that helps us understand and question how things are—and might be.

WRITING EXERCISE TWO: GRAPHIC COLLAGE

Adrian's use of the comic or graphic form as an element in the collage performance 'Four Words' draws on what comic theorist Scott McCloud calls the "magic and mystery" of the 'gutter,' or the space between panels of the comic (1994, p. 66). As we note above, collage processes rely on readers and audiences to put the disparate and fragmented elements of collage into a meaningful whole (p. 63). McCloud calls the process of "observing the parts but perceiving the whole" *closure*, noting that this meaning-making process is an 'agent of change, time, and motion' (p. 65). Moving back and forth between 'cell' and 'gutter', Adrian's performance hovers in the 'liminal', or 'in-between' space of the death, introducing the passage of time and the motion of bodies (from one cell to the next, from basketball court to hospital bed, from spring to Christmas and connecting the elements of body, time and space to the movement of his emotions. Consider a text you've written for one of the exercises in Chapters Two or Three—for example, 'Creating a Character from a News Item' or 'Making People With Words' or 'Smell It Like It Is'. Now:

1. Create three comic cells. Tell your story by drawing it in comic form, paying attention to what you put in the cells and what you leave in the 'gutter.'
2. Create six comic cells and tell the same story again.
3. Create nine cells and tell the same story a third time.
4. Choose one version of your story (three, six, or nine cells) and re-draw it, this time, leaving out some details to fill in 'in performance' as Adrian did with 'Four Words'.
5. Now, share your 'performance' of the comic with someone else (or a group of someone elses), followed by the three-, six-, and nine-cell versions.

6. Have a conversation with your someone else(s). What is gained and lost by expanding the stories? What is gained or lost by adding some of the elements to the cells in performance? Which story is the most moving? Leaves the most up to the audience/reader? Creates the most interesting interpretations?
7. Begin again, this time with another text.

EXEMPLAR THREE: *LOST AND FOUND*

In addition to the chance methods promoted by Tzara, Burroughs, and other contemporary poets and writers, you can approach collaging in a more deliberate way. As an example, take Gertrude Stein's collage approach to creating *Tender Buttons: Objects, Food, Rooms*, which is composed as a series of prose poems that juxtapose everyday objects with descriptive language. Stein's goal was to create "a word relationship between a word and the things seen" (Perloff, 1996). The relationship between word and thing (word and world) is an approach to writing that combines powers of observation with the powers of association advocated by collage techniques. As another example—one that includes drawing images as Adrian's 'Four Words' performance above—consider anthropologist Michael Taussig's (2011) book I *Swear I Saw This: Drawings in Field Notebooks, Namely My Own*. Here, Taussig uses drawings, newspaper clippings, watercolor paintings, and field observations to create textual meditations on the workings of memory; the process of 'translation' between images, experiences, and words; and thousands of people murdered by paramilitary groups in Columbia between 2002 and 2010 (where Taussig has conducted much of his anthropological fieldwork). He creates a relationship between word and thing, asking

> …what am I doing? I really don't know. I am no art critic or historian, or certainly not much of a drawer. All I can say in my defense is that the text pretty much wrote itself as a continuous reaction to that one image. Sometimes I tell people it's like lifting off the layers of an onion, one after the other—a familiar image, after all. But it is more accurate to say I was drawn along. (p. xii)

Stacy has used Taussig's writing, along with Stein's technique of creating 'word relationships' between language and things seen, felt, and heard in poetic texts she's written about adoption. In 'Lost and Found' (2011) several *things*—the recurring appearance of suitcases, phone calls, and letters—

connect seemingly disparate stories about philosopher Walter Benjamin's disappearance and death and Stacy's experience of losing the possibility of adopting a child:

Cartera Grande

... Upon learning that the woman who crossed the French and Spanish border with Benjamin was living in Chicago, [anthropologist Michael] Taussig called her from a pay phone. She knew—or thought she knew—the reason for Taussig's call. He was after Benjamin's case—a large handbag, a *cartera grande*—his only baggage. Benjamin lugged this heavy black case over the Pyrenees, chanting, "I cannot risk losing it ... it is the manuscript that *must* be saved. It is more important than I am" (Taussig, 2006, p. 9). After Benjamin's death, the authorities found and cataloged the *cartera grande* and its contents—a pocket watch, a pipe, a pair of glasses in nickel frames, several photographs, an x-ray, some papers and money—but no manuscript. And, as Taussig reminds, "no body either." (Taussig, 2006, p. 9)

No body, no great

work, no words. Just a suitcase

full of emptiness,

full of the collected pain of the past. Full of fragments of stories ...

Hold

He insists: *you* call

the social worker and say,

"the adoption's off."

You agree, trying to diffuse [your husband's] anger and sadness and ignore your own. But each time you pick up the phone to call, the recriminating sound of the dial tone taunts you. You push the receiver back into its cradle ... You settle on a letter. In it, you say without explanation that you have some things to work out before moving forward. Unable to let go of wanting this relationship ...in spite of knowing the irreconcilable losses she will suffer as your daughter ... you ask to place the adoption on hold. (pp. 328–329)

Call Waiting

Before his death, before the discovery of his missing name, missing body, missing grave, missing briefcase, missing manuscript, and missing *life,* Benjamin made four phone calls and wrote one letter

(Yates, 2010, n.p.). No one knows whom he was calling or whether he got any answers; no one received his parting text, except by delayed delivery (Yates, 2010, n.p.). No one, that is, but Benjamin and even this knowledge has vanished, disappeared. Still, not knowing does not stop you from looking for who and what is gone, for writing in and over lost texts, trying to understand. Not knowing keeps you waiting for the phone to ring, waiting for the call—of adoption, of death, of story, of what's possible. (pp. 331–332)

When Stacy started writing this performative text about the decision to not adopt a second child, she was reading Walter Benjamin's ideas about the storyteller and accounts of his exile, mysterious death and missing manuscript and briefcase. She did not know if or how these stories were related, but she did not press herself to figure out *why* she was writing what she was writing. Instead, she wrote by collaging together fragments that included suitcases, phone calls, and letters until she recognized a way to thread together the fragments of text/experience (for other examples of this kind of writing, see Holman Jones, 2005, 2009, and 2014).

WRITING EXERCISE THREE: NOT-SO-CHANCE COLLAGE[1]

To create a not-so-chance collage similar to Stein's, or Stacy's 'Lost and Found' essay, you can begin by gathering objects, sounds, and texts that have caught your attention for some reason—perhaps you've noticed an object in a new way or you find yourself humming the same tune again and again, or you keep returning to re-read a poem or a passage in a book. Select materials that speak to you emotionally, intellectually, or politically; the ideas are exciting, complex, or frustrating; the writing is compelling; or because the items seem to have some connection to feelings you want to evoke or the experiences you want to write about. Then:

1. Consider the objects, sounds, or texts, writing descriptions or narratives as they occur to you or by simply typing passages that you've underlined or noted.
2. Consider each item one by one or work with multiple sources at one time, building a collection of passages or poems or inventory-like entries.
3. Look over this collection, connecting and grouping—collaging—the disparate material in ways that make sense to/interest you.
4. Do this collaging until you feel inspired to begin writing a scene or narrative, taking the collaged idea(s) as a starting point. Alternatively, if

you're already writing scenes/narratives, look for moments to connect the writing you've done through doubling, juxtaposition, or repetition.

5. Stay open and pay attention to the emerging logic of your choices, thinking about what connects the scenes and narratives you're writing.

Over time, your collaging will develop into an internal through-line. This through-line could be anything—a recurring character, object, feeling, space, or place (such as a shopping bag or the rhythmic click of CD cases or a hospital respirator); a repeated line (textual, musical, or other, such as 'Dear Pa,' or 'click-click-click'); a series of variations on an theme or structure (such as collecting, the number 13 or the addition of the color red into a black and white environment). Use this through-line/logic as you continue to develop your writing project.

EXEMPLAR FOUR: *AT THE SEAMS*

Adrian was also involved in Performance Ensemble, a collective of performers Stacy works with to make original work dedicated to creating social justice. *At the Seams*, an ensemble performance about witnessing violence, was a collage of films, movement pieces, images, and texts on the violence that individuals and collectives bring to each other and to the world based on biases associated with race, class, gender, sexuality, geography, ability, size, etc. The ensemble began their work by reading essays, poetry, and philosophy texts on and about violence and writing narratives and poetry in response to these readings. Adrian offered the poem 'Embrace the Chaos' about his experience as a young soldier in Afghanistan, which includes the lines:

The closing caskets, sleepless nights
Unwanted decisions, maniacal fights
The conflicting roles of accepted values
Constant uncertainty of what you might lose…

I just wish you would sing your blues to a willing ear
There are people that love you, you know?
And you have such a lovely voice
So sing! …
They'll listen, I promise…

I've seen you rise above the clouds
Just to kiss the moon with your fingertips…

Adrian also volunteered to direct a scene in the performance based on this text. He wanted the work to have weight and volume—to function as a material manifestation of the experience of war, both personally as well as socially and politically and to include word, sound, and movement. He began by choreographing a movement piece that opened with Adrian and several other performers moving in pairs behind a veil of darkness—represented by a white scrim lit from behind so that it illuminates their fractured and violent dance (set designed by Adolfo Lagomasino).

Figure 2. Adrian Amor in at the seams. Photo by Rena Petrello

As the performance progressed, Adrian is drawn out into a brightly lit but narrow walkway filled with people (the audience). He struggles to communicate with them and with the outside world, which we can see through large second-story windows. As Adrian pounds his fist on the windows in frustration, we see a figure (Davale Horne) come into view outside: He is both the mirror and the opposite of Adrian—his white clothes and black skin reflect and refract Adrian's black clothes and brown skin.

The windows are inscribed with the text of a collage poem, 'Falling Back Toward Night.' We placed the poem on the glass using vinyl transfer material, so the letters became three-dimensional objects, floating on the glass. Adrian traced his fingers along the letters as he (and the audience) read the poem:

Figure 3. Adrian at the window. Photo by Rena Petrello

Falling Back Toward Night

Falling back toward night.
Biting, scratching
        fighting still.
Unable to take flight.

But look. . .
The wheel of suffering
        lifts itself
on the rhythm of his breathing.

Wind becomes an aria.
your name sings the blues
        to a willing ear.

Kiss the moon with your fingertips.
We'll listen.

This poem was created by collaging Adrian's 'Embrace the Chaos' with portions of Carolyn Forche's 'The Recording Angel' and Nelly Sachs's 'But Look.' All three poems are what Forche describes as "poetry of

Figure 4. 'Falling back toward night' in at the seams.
Photo by Rena Petrello

witness"—that is, poetry that exists in the social space between the personal (emotional, particular, individual but not outside of history) and the political (public, partisan, critical, communal). Forche argues that locating poetry in this third space allow us to the social as a place of resistance and struggle. She writes, "A poem that calls us from the other side of a situation of extremity… might be our only evidence that an event has occurred: it exists for us as the sole trace of an occurrence… Poem as trace, poem as evidence" (1993, p. 17).

'Falling Back Toward Night' is the trace—the element of evidence—of the struggle depicted in the dance and in Adrian's struggle to call out to the other side of his experience of war. The poem formed a meeting place for the two performers (Adrian on the inside and Davale on the outside) to meet each other and to move together in that struggle. The performance is another example of how creating collage texts and collaging performance elements allows us to focus on and make the most of the 'thingness' of texts and writing for performance, as well as how we might see things differently.

WRITING EXERCISE FOUR: CENTO

The cento collage technique can be used to create all manner of texts. From the Latin word for 'patchwork', cento texts are formed entirely by quoting lines from other sources. This technique has been used by writers ranging from Homer and Virgil to Emily Dickinson and Sylvia Plath ('Poetic Form: Cento'). The resulting texts make the most of the collage features of doubleness, juxtaposition, and repetition to create centos that are full of humor and irony. For example, we created the following cento poem using texts by Wendy Chen, Nikki Giovanni, Amy Lowell, Mary Oliver, Sylvia Plath, Adrienne Rich, and Stevie Smith.

Stone and Water Cento

Let the soft animal of your body
love what it loves
dash you in the rain
blend into the beach
dive into the hold
into flaws like a jewel, treasures that prevail.

Lie back and laugh, and let the green-white
water, the sun-flawed beryl water,
flow out much further than you thought.

Meanwhile the sun and the clear pebbles of the rain
are moving across the landscapes.
Black lake, black boat, two black, cut-paper people
they are round and flat
and full of dark advice
not waving, but drowning.

Was the water dark or full of light?
A deep pact between stone and water,
it was all they needed to survive.

THINGS AND...

This chapter has asked you to consider the 'thingness' of the texts we write for performance. In other words, to explore not only the symbols of performance are things are themselves alive and performative, but also how performance is made of and in relation to those things. And just as words are not created or performed without bodies, things do not occur outside of history, time, and space. In the next chapter, we shift our focus to questions of space—the spaces we choose and create in our writing, as well as how our writing creates textual spaces we can enter into, experience, and inhabit.

CHAPTER 4

NOTE

[1] This section is adapted from a discussion of collage techniques in *Autoethnography* (2015) by Adams, Jones & Ellis.

SPACES

WRITING SPACES

Performance happens in space and time and because of this space is a central theme or question in performance (Levan, 2005, p. 120). Bodies, texts, objects, histories, and worlds move, breathe, shift, and change according to their location in space. And whether the space of the performance is a theatre, a street, a hallway, a train platform or an online 'platform', when we write for performance we do so in and through considerations of space. Perhaps the first consideration of space in performance happens when we choose a space in which to write, a workspace. Some writers create workspaces specifically for writing—offices, attic retreats, the (almost mythical) writer's cabin in the woods. Others choose specific environments in which to write—with or without music, in public spaces, in their homes (kitchens, living rooms), or in the world (in cafes or coffeehouses, on buses). Writer Alexander Chee gets most of his writing done on trains and jokes that he wishes he could get "a writer's residency from Amtrak on a sleeper car, or an office booth in a café car" (qtd. in Gibson, 2011). Poet, writer, and musician Patti Smith's memoir *M Train* includes space as the grounding force of the daily practice of writing and persevering through grief and writer's block:

> Snow. Just enough snow to scrape off my boots. Donning my black coat and watch cap, I trudge across Sixth Avenue like a faithful postman, delivering myself daily before the orange awning of Cafe 'Ino. As I labour yet again on variations of the poem I'm writing in memory of Roberto Bolaño, my morning sojourn lengthens well into the afternoon. I order Tuscan bean soup, brown bread with olive oil, and more black coffee. I count the lines of the envisioned 100-line poem, *Hecatomb*, now three lines shy. Ninety-seven clues but nothing solved, another cold-case poem. (Smith, 'It's Not So Easy')

Still other writers elect to write in the spaces in which they envision the performance unfolding—in hospital waiting rooms or city parks or family dining rooms—or to place themselves in these contexts imaginatively. Novelist Elizabeth Crane, for example, writes at home, sitting on her couch with the television on, noting, "It's not very exciting to the onlooker," but it is exciting to her because she's creating stories that are set in the places she's seeing on TV (qtd. in Gibson, 2011).

PERFORMANCE SPACES

Theatres and stages are also workspaces—spaces in which the work of performance will happen. What is necessary for the work of performance to begin? In the classic *The Empty Space*, theatre director Peter Brook writes, "I can take any empty space and call it a bare stage. A man [sic] walks across this empty space whilst someone else is watching him, and this is all that is needed for an act of theatre to be engaged" (1968, p. 9). Though we can think of the workspace of performance as more than an empty, or bare stage; rather, we can consider performance space alive and in motion—a creative and contributing component of the performance process. Writing about entering the space of the theatre, performance scholar and artist Craig Gingrich-Philbrook reminds us that "the space doesn't open like a wonderland in a pop-up storybook, ready made, fully furnished and populated before me. Crossing into it is just the beginning" (Gingrich-Philbrook, 2014, p. 29). In other words, we don't enter theatre (or other performance) spaces, texts in hand, determined and sure in the work we will make (the performance we will give). Instead, crossing the threshold into a performance space is itself a process of creating, of writing. Gingrich-Philbrook continues: "I cross the threshold into the space and the space crosses the threshold into me, or what I think of as me. A workspace and open-source code of influential sub-routines, algorithms, and experiences that/"who" continues the labor of producing variations upon its material through interaction with the environment" (2014, p. 29).

Collaborators Katie Pearl and Lisa D'Amour (PearlDamour) make work that purposefully incorporates interaction with environments, combining narrative; the accumulation of texts, images, and objects; and architectural elements (pearldamour.com). Their goal is to make audiences "feel like they are inside of an experience, rather than watching something happen 'over there'" (pearldamour.com). Their show, *How to Build a Forest* (a collaboration with visual artist Shawn Hall), begins on an empty stage each day. Over the course of eight hours, an entire forest is built, stands complete, and is disassembled. Audiences are invited into the space at any time over the course of the performance, watching from fixed seats or locating themselves inside the forest, and staying for as long as they like. The space itself becomes key element or player in the performance, providing the ground on which the creation and description of environments (such as the old-growth trees destroyed by Hurricane Katrina in 2005 or the ecosystems devastated by the BP oil spill in 2010, both in New Orleans) intersect with the "creative and destructive processes" of our lives as artists and human beings (pearldamour.com). Further, the performance lives on in virtual space, where you can watch a time-lapse video of *How to Build a Forest* as it was created and disassembled at its premier at The Kitchen in New York at: https://vimeo.com/32998219.

The Chicago-based Goat Island performance ensemble also view space as an interactive environment that is central to the work of making performance, particularly what they term an 'encounter area' and 'spaces between.' Their encounter area is a basketball court in a church gym that serves as a rehearsal and performance space. For each work, the group marks out a performance area on the playing area of the court with tape. The tape foregrounds the performance space and backgrounds (without erasing or disguising) the basketball court. It also creates a stage for the encounter between the space, the performers, and the audience. Director Lin Hixson writes, "Eight performance works now sit in the basketball court. The floor holds the worn away remains of 15 years of work" (qtd. in Bottoms & Goulish, 2007, p. 30). The idea of spaces between asks us to imagine the space of performance in an unexpected, simple or 'poor' (that is, without the elaborate sets, lighting, seating, curtains one might expect in a theatre), or neglected space. For example, in much of our teaching work, space and budget limitations have meant that students do not have access to traditional theatre or black box performance spaces. Instead, they've looked to the spaces in between theatre venues and other campus buildings including stairwells, study alcoves, public toilets, and elevators as spaces for staging their performances.

However, staging performances in such 'nontraditional' places requires creativity, flexibility, and thoughtful consideration of the choice of space. For example, we have worked with several students interested in making work that addresses the blurry boundary between 'work' and 'home', and 'life at school' and 'life in the real world'. In one instance, a student transferred the contents of his home office to an elevator in a campus building. Throughout a 24-hour period, he asked people entering the elevator to listen to portions of the books he was reading and papers he was writing for his courses during their rides up and down the building landscape. In another performance, a couple moved the entire contents of their bedroom into a study alcove, where they worked at their writing, watched television, slept, and made love over the course of one week. In both cases, the unexpected spaces of encounter for the performance created curiosity and caused controversy. The performance staged in the elevator was reported to campus security, who removed the student and his belongings with the admonition that the homeless (including students) were not permitted to live in non-designated spaces on campus. The performance staged in the study alcove was reported to the building guarding and campus safety officials, who said that the performance disrupted the work of overnight cleaning crews and that the large amounts of paper in the space (books and the reams of paper piled on and scattered around the desk) created an unreasonable fire hazard. In addition, the performers themselves found that they had difficulty concentrating and sleeping with people moving through their space, looking in drawers, asking questions, and attempting to vacuum around them in the night.

In addition to explaining why and how the work of performance 'belongs' in elevators and other non-traditional spaces, your writing must also take into account alternative staging choices. We write in Chapter Seven about transitioning *Heavier Than Air* from an in-the-round performance space into a proscenium venue and the changes in the text that this transition required (most notably reworking the 'games' scenes from movement-based interactive encounters to more stationary activities). In addition, when performers work in the round or in other irregular spaces (elevators, hallways, outdoors), it becomes difficult to hear text spoken by performers whose backs may be to audience members. In this case, the texts you create might include elements of repetition—repeating texts and movements in multiple directions or multiple spaces so that audiences don't 'miss' the action. This, however, doesn't have to introduce a deficit or redundancy to the performance text. Instead, much like the features of collage described in Chapter Four, repetition creates spaces for new ways of experiencing and making meaning, turning our attention to the rhythms and relationships among elements of the performance. Repetition also allows audiences to see, hear, and experience the same elements of the performance from different vantage points and at different times.

Repetition, along with doubleness and juxtaposition (again, referencing the elements of collage methods) is also a component of performance works that move from in-person to virtual spaces or that incorporate both spaces at once. Here the virtual isn't a space removed from reality or the 'live' body (Chavasta, 2005), but rather a space 'between' in which performers repeat, extend, juxtapose, and double the space-performer-audience encounter. Steve Dixon, a member of the performance collective Chameleons Group, underscores the collage nature of digitally mediated performance, noting that the group's use of both space and stage "enables the live performer to act out a character and narrative on stage whilst inhabiting a wholly different persona on screen. The screen... [allows] simultaneous expression of the external and the internal, the social and the primitive, the conscious and the unconscious, the body and its double" (Dixon, n.d., n.p.).

The Goat Island performance collective and filmmaker Lucy Cash have collaborated to create digital works that are both companions to and distinct works from the 'live' performances. Their collaborative work *A Last, A Quartet* begins with material of the collective's final performance *The Lastmaker* to create a four-screen installation that explores the connections and departures between digital and performance spaces. *A Last, A Quartet* uses film to juxtapose space, time, and rhythm by diving the screen into four sections (a forest, an empty auditorium, a moving camera, a double take) (http://www.goatislandperformance.org/film.htm). The resulting performance gives audiences the experience of being part of multiple spaces—inhabiting multiple bodies, texts, objects, histories, and worlds simultaneously (Cull, 2013, p. 211). You can view *A Last, A Quartet* (2009) at https://vimeo.com/78484997.

Crossing the thresholds of performance spaces, whether we do this crossing in-person or virtually, happens, as Gingrich-Philbrook observes, when we make performance, or when "someone reaches out to/into/through you with it" (2014, p. 32). Considering performance spaces as alive and in motion—creative and contributing components of the writing for performance process—helps us understand not only how spaces do the work of texts, but also how texts themselves can become spaces that set "a network of possibilities in motion" (Gingrich-Philbrook, 2014, p. 35).

TEXTS AS SPACES

What if we saw the performance text itself—whether on the page or in space—as an environment in which performance occurs (Blau, 1990, p. 38)? Here, text itself becomes a space of performance and the words we write become spaces in which bodies move and things come alive with meaning (and mean differently). In other words, texts become material and corporeal spaces in performance. Performance studies scholar Della Pollock (1998) tells us that one of the characteristics of such 'performative' writing is that it is evocative—it makes us feel—and that "the page is the material stage" or site for that creation of feeling (p. 82). As we noted in Chapter Three, performative protest movements like *#BlackLivesMatter* incorporate both text as material bodies-in-performance, as well as a visual meme for mobilizing and gathering 'actors' for public assembly in diverse spaces.

Conceptual artist Jenny Holzer shows us how words are both material and corporeal, existing in time and space in her text-based visual artworks, which she terms "language as art" ('Jenny Holzer'). While a participant in the Whitey Museum's independent study program, she began experimenting with texts from Eastern literature and philosophy, which she simplified into brief phrases or 'truisms' that she printed and wheat-pasted onto buildings, signs, and telephone booths in New York. The truisms inspired pedestrians to respond to the text by writing messages on the posters. Since then, Holzer has experimented with making words material by projecting texts onto buildings, LED signboards, and city streets—spaces people in which will encounter these texts in their everyday lives (Siegel, 1995; you can see examples of Holzer's projections at: http://projects.jennyholzer.com/projections). Holzer's work makes poetic texts "available and noticeable to a public that has long ignored it" ('Jenny Holzer: Multidisciplinary Dweeb'). Like Holzer's work, which transforms word into world, the following exemplars demonstrate how writing for performance can make texts into spaces that are available and noticeable to an audience.

EXEMPLAR ONE: TIM MILLER'S BODY MAPS

As we discussed in Chapter Three, Anne's play *Surviving Jonas Salt* demonstrates how the lost body is a text and the text is a lost body in performance. We can also write the body as space—as a material territory to be explored and experienced. Performance artist Tim Miller uses the body as a map in his performance work, which charts his experience as a gay man and activist in America in the era of AIDS, marriage equality, and immigration battles. For example in his performance *US*, Tim documents in loving and heartbreaking detail the prospect of being separated from his partner, Australian-born writer Alistair McCartney, due to the refusal of US law and immigration policy to recognize their relationship (and echoes Anne's performance text *Leave to Stay*, presented in Chapter Two). Tim and Alistair perform the following poem (Alistair speaking the first line of each couplet, Tim the second), which reads, in part:

It was the safest I'd felt in years.
His body was so alive under my touch.

Our words give in to a big silence.
I'm off the edge of the map.

Two bodies just trusting.
I am finding my own way… (Miller, 2006, p. 205)

In addition to being a powerful solo performer, Tim is also a masterful workshop facilitator. In his body mapping workshops, Tim encourages participants to first think of their bodies as a landscape that holds stories and then to re-map (and re-story) those landscapes to reveal what's covered over, what's unexpected, what's in need of celebration or healing or gentle touch. When working with a group of five gay men in Birmingham, UK to re-map and re-story their bodies, Tim observes:

I find it very poignant how urgent it is for men, gay men in particular, to get the chance to re-map their bodies…[to] explore this more vulnerable and metaphoric potential body…The menu of potential representations offered to (imposed on) men is so oppressive that the guys in the workshops grab the opportunity to re-imagine their embodiment. I am also reassured that plain folks want to do this—not just performance artists and those inclined to theorize! (2006, pp. 158–159)

In workshop, he begins the body mapping work by first moving the body in space, then drawing the body in space, then telling the body in space by performing the "oral tradition of workshop participant's body map stories. Only then does the writing—which comes out of a "really breath-filled and sweaty place," begin (Miller, 2016, n.p.).

WRITING EXERCISE ONE: BODY MAPPING

As we noted above, Tim Miller's body mapping workshop exercise asks performers to take a fly-over view of their bodies, charting their topographies not in terms of any ideal or expected idea about what gender or sexuality or ability should "look" or feel like, but instead focusing on the actual experience of being inside their bodies. Tim asks the group to consider a number of metaphors and images:

• What animals live in your body? What places?
• What cultures? What histories?
• Map your scars, your broken bones, your tattoos.

- Map your ancestors, memories, desires, and hopes.
- Think of your drawing as your treasure map, your message in a bottle, your love letter to yourself, your dumping ground for feelings, experiences, and things you want to give away/bury.

Following this re-mapping, take another fly-over view, looking at the contours and canyons of the world's you've drawn, honing in on the stories that each part of your body holds (2006, p. 159). Ask:

- What is the story of the elbow? The teeth? The eyes? The genitals?
- What happened to make that scar? That broken bone? That tattoo?
- What part of your body has a story that really *needs* to be told?
- Is there a place on your body that carries a story so important that if it doesn't it told you might burst? (2006, pp. 159–160).

Look at your map and consider some of our culture's most persistent body metaphors as fully as possible. Our daily language is full of these metaphors:

- *He has feet of clay*
- *I was caught red-handed*
- *He broke my heart*
- *My head is in the clouds* (p. 160).
- *I am walking on eggshells*
- *My heart is a stone*

Let the associations sparked by these metaphors leap forward, uncensored, as you tell the story of the place on your body that needs to be told. Dig deep and find the metaphor and the story of transformation that comes from this place (p. 160). Now, find a physical action that expresses this story. Perform the action as you tell someone else your story.

Tim notes that stories that come up and out of the maps of our bodies are "rich with metaphor and urgency," and telling, performing and "and having them witnessed adds to their resonance" (p. 162).

Ryan Haddad is an actor, writer, and solo performer whose work explores the complicated intersection of romance and disability from his perspective as a gay man with cerebral palsy (ryanjhaddad.com; for more on disability and queer in theatre, see the work of playwright John Belluso). Ryan's solo performance *Hi, Are You Single?* is an extension of work he began with Tim at Ohio Wesleyan. Out of that workshop and the mapping exercises in it, Ryan developed the full-length solo performance, from which the following excerpt is drawn. This brief section shows—without telling—how Ryan's body is mapped and understood by others—in ways that differ radically from his own body story:

> ...He was. So. Hot. Tall and Strong, at least according to his profile and the Facebook stalking I had done. So when my parents left town the next week, I asked him to come over.

> "*What's your address?*" he texted back.

> "First I want to confirm one thing. It's okay that I have cerebral palsy, right? As if I had to as his permission.

> "*What?*" he replied.

> "I have cerebral palsy. That's why there's a walker in my pic. You never asked me about it, so I assume you don't care."

> "*I thought that was from a play you were in.*"

> "Good guess, but it's mine. The CP just limits the mobility in my legs and weakens my arms a little. Everything else is fine."

> "*I'm sorry man,*" he said, "*I can't be cool with that.*"

> Well. That would have absolutely devastated me, if he could spell. But he wrote I-k-a-n-no-apostrophe-t-b-k-o-o-l-w-d-a-t"... So we weren't taking boyfriend material here, but it did sting. You know, it wasn't until I started trying to meet guys that I ever had to confront my cerebral palsy like that. Honestly I can only remember a few times growing up when I have to face any sort of discrimination. In third grade, a girl named Samantha called me a cripple. That bitch. On my first day of high school, the special ed teacher assumed I was going to be in her classes, even though I was scheduled for all honors. Some friends avoided socializing with me on weekends because they didn't want to deal with the responsibility, or burden. But I never gave those things much thought. It never even occurred to me that my disability might make being gay a little more complicated. Which is why I was really confused the day after I came out when my mother hugged me, crying, and said, "*I'm scared. Now you're different in two ways.*"

A.B. a poet, performer, and scholar developed the following narrative based on her body mapping work with Tim. Here, A.B.'s body is mapped within the cold space of a bathroom as she struggles to "lift this heavy body" off of the floor, striving to face herself in the mirror, and affirm her reflection:

Off My Knees

Today I am 26
It's my birthday
I have asked my family to barbecue

But now I am here…
Bent before this porcelain altar

I have become accustomed to gagging on
Blunt objects
I have bowed before the same godless idols
Since I was 16
I don't want to be here…
This isn't who I am
I am this body
This heavy body…
But lifting this body all these years has made me strong…

I have been taking a poetry class the last four weeks
We have been doing daily affirmations
Mine are written on my mirror
From the floor I read

I am beauty
I am wisdom
I am art
I am love

I am starting to believe it

Sometimes is more difficult to swallow the truth about ourselves than to
taste the spew of our self loathing

In class we say these things

I am beauty
I am wisdom
I am art
I am love

I am starting to believe it

Today I accept the perfection of my artistry and allow it to unfold in the
way that it does

A.B.'s poem writes her body in space—it is a body that heaves and is heavy, that is both uncertain and strong. Her poem also performs text as space—in this case, the affirmations, written on the bathroom mirror, speak and are repeated; they become a mantra that A.B. is "starting to believe."

EXEMPLAR TWO: *AFFIRMING SELVES IN POETRY*

When Stacy teaches writing for performance, she asks students to 'materialise poetry' by writing poems that deal in some sense with space—landscapes, buildings, or psychological or emotional spaces; the movement of bodies; and/or physical manifestations of language and ideas through projections, sculpture, paintings, or some other 'canvas.' The goal of this work is to make poetry "available and noticeable" to readers and audiences. This is an illustration of how writing for performance, particularly when we take our texts into unexpected spaces—spaces where it might matter most, when people are confronting their images and their lives, before them, in word and world—can help us see and embody things differently.

As an example of materializing poetry, Stacy and A.B. created *Affirming Selves in Poetry*, featuring the work of spoken word artists Natalie Patterson, Carrie Rudzinzki, Joel Jaimes, and Adrian Amor. Inspired by A.B.'s work with Tim Miller (above), the project was designed as a continuation of "Mirrorless Monday," a project designed to promote awareness eating disorders and promote positive body image that involved covering the mirrors in the women's bathroom on our college campus during the last week of February (part of the US National Eating Disorders Awareness Week). *Affirming Selves* was installed in April during US National Poetry Month and featured spoken word poems that show the writers/narrators exploring their own versions of positive selves. Instead of covering the mirrors, the poetry was transferred to vinyl cutout and mounted to the surfaces (tiled walls, mirrors, and metal stalls) in both the men's and women's bathrooms. In this project, poetry was materialized in the move from the page into three-dimensional space. And by retaining the reflective surfaces in the bathrooms, those who entered were able to see themselves *inside* the poetry. For example, Carrie Rudzinzki's Poem, 'The Prayer' asks viewers to see themselves in the words, "My god, my God, I am a stupid, selfish prayer/Your voice has begun to sound like my own voice/and I haven't yet learned to silence my own fears." The poem continues:

89

My god, my god
I have eaten my reflection
So many times and I am still hungry

My god
I have been called "sir"
Enough times to my face
To understand I don't not see myself as beautiful…
My God, My God
I will not apologize for the absence of my own strength
I will forgive myself.
I forgive myself.
I forgive myself.

My God,
I have been my own god,
Forgive me

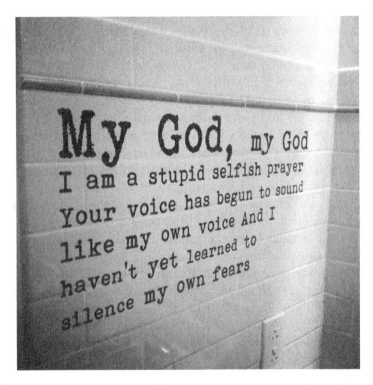

Figure 5. 'The Prayer' in affirming selves in poetry. *Photo by A.B.*

Adrian Amor's poem, 'Embrace the Chaos,' featured in Chapter Four, was also part of the installation. The poem speaks to Amor's experience as a young soldier in Afghanistan, and to the other "young travelers" who encountered the poem in the often uncertain and confronting space of the university.

Embrace the Chaos

Keep your chin up young traveler
Don't let darkness and turbulence discourage you

The closing caskets, sleepless nights
Unwanted decisions, maniacal fights
The conflicting roles of accepted values
Constant uncertainty of what you might lose

And yet here we are, still fighting
Ready and able to take on the unpredictable storms
Stronger than who we were once before
Skin thicker, heart bigger, mind wiser, more experienced than yesterday

Refined perspectives, new objectives,
No longer captives of the shackles that kept our souls from running…
I just wish you would sing your blues to a willing ear
There are people that love you, you know?
And you have such a lovely voice
So sing! …
They'll listen, I promise

You don't always have to wear that cape
Let go, embrace the chaos
Wrap your arms around its shoulder to cry on
Use it to guide your way
I know it's hard, easier said than done
But I've seen you rise above the clouds
Just to kiss the moon with your fingertips

I believe in you…

Where elements of 'Embrace the Chaos' were incorporated in the collage poem, 'Falling Back Toward Night,' the entire poem was featured in the *Affirming Selves* installation. In the unexpected space of bathroom, the mirror becomes a space of encounter, the words "I believe in you" joining the materiality of the text-as-space with the 'you' (reader/audience member) looking into the mirror.

WRITING EXERCISE TWO: THE TOWN

Writing space asks us to think of the texts we create as material, corporeal entities—as rivers and mirrors; territories and towns. The following exercise, adapted from Rachel McKibbens's exercise of the same name poetry writing workshop, asks you to write into space, discovering the geography of experience through the metaphor of a town (see Rachel's website for hundreds of poetry writing exercises: http://rachelmckibbens.blogspot.com.au).

Choose one of the towns from the list below. The condition of the town should be based on its name. Write the atmosphere of the town, starting with the ecology (relationships among animals and plant life), then considering the architecture (roads, buildings, houses, lighting) and then turn to the people who inhabit the town. Make sure you provide yourself with as many details as possible. Next, answer the following questions: What thrives in a town like this? Who or what is its mayor? What is considered a crime? What is considered a gift? What is the soundtrack? What is the sky filled with? What runs in the rivers and streams? What is empty or vacant? What is too plentiful?

Use the description to generate a scene, monologue, or poem about your town, focusing on the rhythms, repetitions, spatial relations, and kinds of 'attention' you want to create. Possible names for your town might include:

The Town of Forgetting
The Town of Hunger
The Town of Hollow Women/Hollow Men
The Town of Misunderstanding
The Town of Unclaimed Children
The Town Without Death
The Town of Missing Soldiers
The Town of Gossips
The Town of Superstition
The Town of Absent Parents
The Town Without Sadness
The Town of Lost Dogs

SPACES AND...

In this chapter, we've asked you to consider not only the spaces in which you do your own writing for performance, but also how space shapes that writing and how writing creates a space and fills it with words, bodies, and things. The collaborative dance among words, bodies, things, and spaces doesn't end with your writing, however. Instead, these four pivots are central to the process of moving your work from the page to the stage. In the next chapter, we turn our attention to getting your work 'on its feet', beginning with the processes of rehearsing and devising.

REHEARSING/DEVISING

RESEARCH INTO PERFORMANCE

In this chapter we focus on rehearsing and devising, using as our exemplar the workshop performance of *Out/In Front: Teaching Change*. This performance began its life in the scripting of a series of in-depth research interviews that we transitioned into a devised workshop performance. The play then took on a new life as a (further devised and) scripted play titled *Heavier Than Air*. In this chapter, we profile *the Out/In Front* performance and our efforts to find the best theatrical form for the research data on which the play is based. We discuss the origins of our devising; considerations about what kind of 'message' we wanted to convey; which focused on honour the words and lived experiences of the interviewees; and the kinds of feedback we expected to receive from our audience, which was composed primarily of drama educators and researchers gathered for a conference in Singapore. In addition to sharing strategies for shaping the work and creating a draft of the 'final' Singapore performance script, we include a step-by-step account of the 'how to' of transforming straight-up interview transcripts into a performance script that an audience wants to see, is moved by, and can make sense of. In doing so, we share some of the original interview transcripts so readers can see how they changed in order to create the *Out/In Front* script, as well as some of our devising and thinking process as we rehearsed the play for performance. In this way, our discussion of *Out/In Front* contributes to the growing body of research on arts based research processes and practice-led research as scholarly endeavour (Sinclair & Harris, 2016).

FORM AND CONTENT

There are a wide range of related forms and terminology for talking about the work of turning research data into performance. For *Out/In Front*, we created an ethnographically-informed playscript. As we will discuss throughout Chapters Six and Seven, all ethnographically-informed drama scripts are not the same—in their making or in their methodological homes and traditions. Ethnographically-informed performances are described using a range of names: *ethnodrama and ethnotheatre* (Leavy, 2015; Ackroyd & O'Toole,

2010; Saldana, 2005), *performance ethnography* (Alexander, 2005; Conquergood, 1991, 2001; Madison, 2012; Spry, 2011), *verbatim theatre* (Hare, 2009; Kaufman & Tectonic Theatre, 2000; Deavere Smith,1992; Rickman & Viner, 2006), *research-informed theatre* (Belliveau & Lea, 2016), and other versions of adapting both new and found data into fictionalised or semi-fictionalised performance works (see, for example, the Australian theatre-in-education play *Blackrock* by Nick Enright, 1999).

No matter what context or process you might settle upon, when adapting research data into performance texts, writers always write with an audience in mind. Performance writing is, at its heart, a conversation between the performers and the audience, and while this can also be said of (some, though not all) research, writing for performance is defined by this characteristic and impetus. Therefore, let's begin with form: this exemplar cannot strictly be considered an example of verbatim theatre in that we intentionally altered the words of the interviews in a number of ways in service to the story's and the play's dramatic power/potential. We feel it's an effective exemplar for this book in part for that very reason. Those new to practice-led research can sometimes become constrained by a false notion that research methods fall into strict categories that are mutually exclusive. This is a myth. While it is absolutely vital to commit to the investigative and ethical practices of any method, writing for performance encourages practitioner-researchers to experiment, with a commitment to the work and a respect for performance above all else. Sharing the work you create with an audience is your ultimate goal. In that spirit, we outline the performance project which has gone through many incarnations and many names, but first referred to as *Out/In Front* (or, affectionately and colloquially as *Queer Teachers*).

RAW MATERIAL: THE RESEARCH PROJECT

Out/In Front: Teaching Change had its inaugural workshop performance in Singapore in July 2015. We devised the play from transcripts of research interviews with Australian teachers conducted during a mixed method research study in 2013 by the co-researchers Anne Harris, Emily Gray, and Tiffany Jones. The study consisted of 63 online surveys sourced via FaceBook, and 14 interviews with teachers in the Australian state of Victoria. Emily, Tiffany, and Anne did not want the study to focus solely on the 'difficult' experiences of queer teachers—experiences we had all experienced or known of, because we felt focusing only on these stories reinforced negative stereotypes about 'tragic gay teachers'. So, in the original research study design we included questions concerning both the positive and challenging aspects of being an LGBTIQ-identified teacher in a primary or secondary school in Australia, and referenced studies in England, Ireland, and other countries on the same topic which was ultimately developed into the edited collection *Queer Teachers, Identity and Performativity* (Harris & Gray, 2014).

After we interviewed the teachers, we performed a thematic analysis and coded transcripts based on those themes. We then segregated the quotations in a 3-stage process that resulted in different 'sorts' of the material: all ages, sexualities, and gender identities together to see the breadth of our research participants; mapping and other visual schema to see themes present across the transcripts; a compilation of each teacher's 'main' story plus salient quotes. We gained ethics for both the online-sourced surveys (using FaceBook and SurveyMonkey) and the in-person interviews.

We created a 'community' page to solicit participants for the survey and interview. We also used our LGBTIQ annual festival in Melbourne, and snowball sampling (where participants refer other potential participants to the researchers), to gain additional interview participants. We had 63 responses in total, and 31 agreed to be interviewed in person. Ultimately, fourteen were interviewed, and from there, we analysed nine of the full transcripts. This is the raw material that formed the basis of *Out/In Front*.

THE ADAPTATION PROCESS

After the initial study was completed by Anne, Emily, and Tiffany, about a year passed before Anne and Stacy had the idea of adapting the material for a performance piece. Anne began the adaptation process, editing the original transcripts in various ways ranging from altering prepositions, pronouns, and brief non-sequiturs, to merging these ethnographic narratives into a few performable characters who, together, could take the audience on a journey of diversity (of both identity and experience). In keeping with the researcher's original commitment to representing queer teaching lives as not one thing, and as not all difficult knowledges, Anne and Stacy's adaptation focused on showing what had emerged in the interviews themselves: that things were both improving but also had a long way still to go.

At the time of the original interviews (2013), study participants had the opportunity to pick their own pseudonym by which they would be identified. 'Catalin' became Kaz in the play. Others left it up to us. As in scholarly publishing (with the exception, at times, of visual research), we chose pseudonyms and created characters that were not related to the participants (to ensure 'anonymity'). In many cases, however, the teachers interviewed wanted to be identified, wanted to stay involved, and were deeply gratified to be able to share their stories—stories that in some cases had remained a silent burden for too long.

In the next section we will contrast some of the original interview transcripts with the script that we eventually developed for the Singapore performance. Following that we will detail the ways in which we staged the workshop performance and the feedback we received, highlighting some particular ways of devising performance as you go through a rehearsal/ workshop period. Finally we will share the full script of *Out/In Front* as it existed for Singapore, which in Chapter Seven can be contrasted with the script that we used for full production of *Heavier Than Air* in the Adelaide Feast Festival late in 2015.

THE WORKSHOP PERFORMANCE

We recognised the upcoming International Drama in Education Research Institute (IDIERI) conference in Singapore would be a good context to share an early version of the work, and we submitted the following abstract:

Performing Ourselves: LGBTIQ Teachers Out/In Front

Anne Harris (Monash University) and Stacy Holman Jones (Monash University)

With the explosion of the field of sexualities research with students and young people, it was only a matter of time until researchers turned our eyes to the experiences of lesbian, gay, bisexual, transgender and queer-identified teachers. This performance is an excerpt of a full-length play developed from the transcripts of teacher interviews in an ethnographic study of LGBTIQ teachers. This performance session involves presenting a sample of the show, plus a discussion of the ways in which the work of adapting ethnographic transcripts to performance (not in itself new) is evolving into multimedia, multimodal forms that themselves challenge research paradigms and presentational forms. This session therefore asks audience members to critically consider the 'performance' of being an LGBTIQ teacher in today's schools, but also the research implications of performing ourselves in research contexts. The structure and performance style of the play strategically uses theatrical elements including soundscape, lighting, and silhouette/shadow to highlight the ways in which LGBTIQ teachers remain spectral/partial figures in schools that refuse to invite our 'whole selves' in. Drawing on performance techniques used in the chorale-based 'Not Now, Not Ever!', this proposal hopes to engage attendees in discussion of the sometimes-painful work of 'opening frames' around 'identity, culture and difference' through applied theatre practices.

The Stage

For the performance in Singapore, we were in a black box theatre with about thirty attendees. In lieu of any kind of set (due to the difficulty of transporting materials between Melbourne and Singapore), we developed a series of PowerPoint images and a basic soundscape. When we encountered difficulties getting into the space for a technical rehearsal, the day before the performance we completely changed our approach to the staging: we threw out all the technical elements and proscenium performer/audience mono-directional relationship (see Figure 6), and decided to stage the performance "in the round" in an interactive way with the audience.

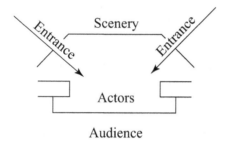

Figure 6. Proscenium stage

This decision illustrates the first rule of rehearsing and performance: be flexible and be ready to change your performance to meet the needs of your audience and the constraints of your space!

We decided we would enter as the first characters, vice principal Mr Hall and trans teacher Dan, as though it was the first day of school, and ask the audience ('drama students') to help us make the chairs into a circle for 'class'. This choice allowed us to immediately immerse the audience in the action we loved, and it implicated them in the worlds of these queer teachers, which we politically felt was important. The audience were not allowed to stay 'outside the circle' as 'innocent bystanders'. We also knew that we wanted to have some seats in the centre of the circle, so that we could perform in/within/around the chairs as a kind of *panopticon* (a term derived for a prison design described by social theorist Jeremy Bentham, in which the cells are arranged around a raised central guard station, from which the prisoners can at all times be observed—even when the guard is not present or cannot be seen, the prisoners 'observe' and 'check' their own behaviour from the point of view of the guard) in keeping with the interview commentary about surveillance and policing within their school experiences as queer teachers.

Once we had reconfigured the room, it looked more like this:

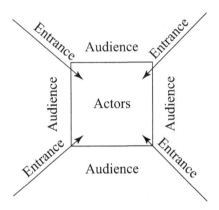

Figure 7. Arena or in-the-round stage

While the audience were reconfiguring the room, we placed sheets of paper on a few of the seats so that we could have empty chairs to occupy and use as props/set for the performance. With this configuration, we played outside around the circle, inside the circle, sitting in the circle, and sitting in the chairs that constituted the inner circle. Creating so many playing spaces allowed us to not only evoke different 'areas' or 'places' in the school but also interact intimately with the audience, moving in and out of them constantly, again never letting them 'off the hook' by keeping their distance.

In addition to this performance tactic, we also quickly brainstormed two 'drama games' that provided interludes to the heavy text-based nature of this piece but also took our ethic of 'pushing' the audience one step further.

Physicalising the Script—The Games

One challenge with a 'talking' play like *Out/In Front* is finding ways to effectively animate it, without the actions seeming 'staged'. With only a few props (a suit jacket, a hat, a scarf), we (who are not primarily performers) had our work cut out for us! So in addition to our simple agit prop staging approach, we included two games to simulate the kinds of heteronormative environments that our queer teachers dealt with every day at work. Only our games were fun (mostly), not distressing like homophobic and transphobic workplaces are for queer teachers.

The first game came about a third of the way into the play. We stopped the action and said, "Okay, everybody up, make a line, everyone in a straight line." We were very teacher-y about it, so they did what they were asked. We then instructed the audience to put themselves in order from least masculine to most masculine. It was, predictably, hilarious, as many 'women' ended up further along the masculine side than the 'men' in the room. Now, we felt as performers we could ask these audience members to do some pretty confronting things like this activity because we were all drama educators and researchers. When we developed this game, we discussed how risky it would be to do it with a more general audience (read more on this in Chapter Six). The Singapore audience members did as they were asked, and we all had a great laugh about it. Following the game they were allowed to sit back down and the show proceeded.

The second game, which we introduced about two-thirds through the performance, was purposely more confronting. This time we asked the audience to stand up again and put themselves in line in order from most 'queer' to most 'straight'. We left them to figure out what those terms meant and how they self-identified. This caused people more confusion, hilarity, and in some cases distress, but after a few minutes the audience had themselves in a line. Then we did something even more risky and confronting: we cut the line in half and said "Okay people at the queer end of the line, and come back into the circle and sit down. People at the straight end of the line, go and stand outside the circle." Everyone complied, though some (both those that returned to the circle and those who were relegated to the outside) were hesitant. We resumed the action of the show with about a dozen people standing outside the circle, directing our performance to only those audience members seated within the circle and ignoring those on the outside. As the performance went on, the discomfort of the 'outsiders' grew. This discomfort was both physical and psychic: it was a powerful enactment of being 'left out', the kinds of 'microaggressions' that queer teachers reported feeling on a daily basis in their schools.

The last game involved props that emerged spontaneously from the scraps of paper we'd placed the seats to reserve them as playing spaces. One of the audience members, an experienced applied theatre practitioner, was captivated by the scrap of paper on the seat next to her. Throughout the performance, she played with it, folded it, ultimately doodled and wrote things on it. Others followed her lead. When we had the talk back after the show ended, this audience member strongly advocated for the paper to be incorporated into any more developed version of the play. She said she wanted to participate more fully than the physicalizing of the 'lines', that she liked the tactile nature of the paper, and that she felt that because paper is a core 'prop' of teaching and of school environments it should play a larger role in the play. We took her advice and brought the paper idea forward into the full production of Heavier Than Air (more on that in Chapter Seven).

EXCERPTS FROM *OUT/IN FRONT*

Below are just a few excerpts comparing the original transcripts with excerpted passages in the script. What began as fourteen separate interviews became six composite characters. While we tried to keep the dialogue itself as close to the interview transcripts as possible, we changed the gender and sexual orientation of the speakers to represent a wider and more diverse range of queer teachers.

A note on the stage directions in italics in the script: these are production notes that indicate staging of the actors. We mapped the round stage as a clock and our positions as performers as corresponding with the numbers 1–12. Lastly, the in bold text indicates where we spoke lines in unison.

Transcript Excerpt

...So I mean I always feel like it's very hard for me to hide my sexuality. My hair was—well, it's funny like when I knew I was going to become a teacher, sort of 12 months before I started my Dip Ed I started growing my hair longer again so I could fly under the radar a bit and not have to—think I could still get a job and not have to deal with homophobia and trying to get a job. So I started—my hair was pretty short. I grew it long, sort of to about thereish, but I was just like a little lesbian. It was like blind Freddy would have seen it.

Became:

Scene 1: Really Really Short (Kaz, Queer Female Identified Character)

[ANNE plays KAZ stationary at 7 and counter rotation to face the STUDENT, who STACY plays circling outside the circle clockwise.]

Kaz: I've always had really short hair, really quite short hair/
Student: *Do you have a boyfriend Miss?*
Kaz: It's really hard for me to hide my sexuality, see./
Student: *Why do you have short hair?*
Kaz: Well, it's funny like/
Student: *Miss—*
Kaz: When I knew I was going to become a teacher/
Student: *Miss do you have kids?*
Kaz: Twelve months before I started my Dip Ed/
I started growing my hair longer
So I could fly under the radar and not have to/
Student: *Miss – what's your boyfriend's name?*
Kaz: Deal with homophobia/
And try to get a job at the same time.

Kaz: So my hair **was** pretty short.
Student: *Miss, do you have a partner?*
Kaz: I grew it long, sort of to about there-ish, but I was just
so queer!
Student: *Miss—*
Kaz: Blind Freddy would have seen it./
Student: *"Miss, do you have kids?" "How old are you Miss? Do you
have a partner? Do you have a boyfriend Miss?"/*

Kaz: And the very first week at work a student says,
Student: *Miss, why do you have short hair?*
Kaz: And I said, "Why do **you** have short hair?"

Kaz: They're trying to work out the social codes.

Student: *Miss, do you have kids?*
Kaz: Trying to work out what means what
And how it relates to them.
Still. It doesn't stop them.
From going too far.

Kaz: The latest form of harassment
Has been the Year Sevens saying to me in class openly:
Student: *"How old are you Miss, why don't you have kids? Do you
have a partner? Do you have a boyfriend Miss?"*

Transcript Excerpt

And they used to ask if I had a boyfriend over and over again and I just used to say, "No." And then every day they'd go, "Miss, got a boyfriend yet?" and I'd say, "Nuh" and that was all. They never said, "Have you got a girlfriend?" so I just didn't say. Mmm.

Became:

Scene 1: Really Really Short (Kaz)—CONT

Kaz:	That's the constant. Just last week, a girl constantly saying:
Student:	*"Do you have a boyfriend, what's your boyfriend's name?"*

Kaz:	And I, I just ignored it. Tried to redirect. Tried to move on. And she—she just kept asking.
Student:	*"Do you have a boyfriend, what's your boyfriend's name?"*
Kaz:	Would not/
Student:	*"Do you have a boyfriend?*
Kaz:	Stop.
Student:	*"What's your boyfriend's name?"*

Kaz:	In the end I said,
Student:	*Emily. you will have to stop. Because that. is sexual. harassment.*

Kaz:	*[in wonder]* And she did…! *[beat]*
Student:	*[slowly building]* "Oh Miss, "You look like Ellen. She has short hair, just like you. Miss, do you know Ellen miss?"/*

Transcript Excerpt

…depending on the demographic and the location, and the culture, I guess, of the school. I think it comes down to, yeah, location and what kids are exposed to, so—I know when I was at CBC in St Kilda, for example, that's certainly not an affluent school, but it's—those kids come from, I don't know, wealthy families through to high-rise Housing Commission families. But they're exposed to a lot of things, so they've got their head around a lot more than what, say, kids in Bendigo may, in terms of—they haven't had—encountered it, so maybe they haven't processed it or even thought about what they really think. So location, I think, is a determining factor, but I also think demographic certainly is...for those kids, it's not an issue—and I'm not saying that they're all pro-gay rights, some of them certainly are, but they can articulate what they think and what they feel, and they can also discern the logic and arguments on both sides much better.

Became:

Scene 3: 100% Present (Mike, Gay Male-Identified Character)

[ANNE plays MIKE from outside the circle, starting confidently by putting his jacket on and moving further out clockwise as the narrative progresses. STACY plays the STUDENT, heckling from the centre seat at 3.]

Mike: I think it comes down to location, demographics, what kids are exposed to.
—those things influence your experience as a teacher.

I was teaching in St Kilda, for example, in what was certainly not an affluent school—
But they're exposed to a lot of things, a lot more than kids in the country maybe.
To those kids, gayness is just not an issue—and I'm not saying that they're all
pro-gay rights,
Though some of them certainly are—
But they can articulate what they think and what they feel
Can see both sides much better. Because of location
And demographics
And what they're exposed to.

It's taken a long time
15-plus years
To come to terms with my own sexuality.
Its great to now feel so comfortable
Within myself
And with myself
At school.

[STUDENT stops heckling.]

Mike: But I would still say you're never a 100% present
[turns and plays to the circle but from outside it]
As a gay teacher, I'm never 100% present in the room
The way others are able to be
Never 100% there, as a teacher, as a person.
As a gay man.
Never. 100% there.

Transcript Excerpt

That reminds me of another incident that I had where I think a girl was flirting with me in class. She was a Year 10 student, so probably about 15, and she was like, just would always come up and sit on my desk and ask me personal questions. And she would do things like, I remember her grabbing my pencil case. Like she'd just like—and I said, "Give it back," and she'd be like, "No." Like she wanted me to, sort of, chase her. She was being all, you know, just too, sort of, interested and, yeah, playing games with me all the time and she was really annoying. But I also just felt uncomfortable because I thought I think she's a lesbian and maybe she knows that I am and I'm worried that, you know, she shouldn't—I feel like she's crossing over boundaries and I don't want her to but I'm not sure what to do about it 'cause she hasn't said anything that I could actually tell to somebody else to make them believe me. And it might sound like I'm thinking of her in a sexual way if I said something about that, so I wasn't even sure.

Became:

Scene 6: I Didn't Say Anything (Pam, Pansexual Female-Identified Character)

[STACY plays PAM from inside the circle, moving between 9, noon, 3 and 6, with ANNE seated in the inner circle as the female STUDENT at 12.]

Pam: That reminds me of another incident
Where I think a girl was/
Flirting with me in class.

          She was a year 10 student, so probably about 15, 16 years old.
And she would come up/

And sit on my desk/
And ask me personal questions.
And she would
She would do things.

I remember her grabbing my pencil case once.
She grabbed it and I said
Give it back,
And she was all like,

Student: *No.*

Pam: Like she wanted me to, sort of, chase her.
She was just too **interested** and,
Playing games with me all the time. Really annoying.

And I felt uncomfortable because I thought,
Student: She's queer
Pam: And maybe she knows that
I'm queer
And I felt like
she's crossing over boundaries and I didn't—
Didn't want her to

But I wasn't sure what to do about it
'Cause she hadn't
Student: *Said anything*
Pam: Anything I could tell somebody else to make them believe me.
And it might sound like I'm thinking of her in a sexual way
If I said something/
Said anything/
So I didn't.
I just let it go.
I waited for the school year to be over/
And I just let it go.
I didn't say anything.

Transcript Excerpt

And I think it doesn't help as a teacher if you don't share things with the class because the kids when they get to know you better they like you better and…they respond better. Yeah. Makes you a better teacher. So when you withhold things you don't get to have such a good relationship. I had an opportunity, a good opportunity to come out in the class once and I didn't do it. I think the girl who was talking in the class must've been a lesbian, I suppose. What's the statistic about how many people are meant to be gay? Is it one in 10? Yeah. She—there must have been 20, 19 kids in the room or something 'cause we were all just sitting around and she said, "You know the statistics say that two in every 20 people are gay and there's 20 people in this room." And then she just looked at me [laughs] and I was like, "Yeah, that is true." She was like, "I wonder who they are," and she was staring at me and I was like—

Q: Could it be you and me [laughs]?
A: I know. Like she said it really pointedly.
Q: What a coward, what a coward. Those are terrible moments, aren't they?
A: Yeah, I just didn't—I just couldn't do it.
Q: Did the sweat start trickling down [laughs]?
A: I think I'd just gotten so used to dodging questions and things and I just—yeah, I took it in my stride. I didn't mind. I thought it was funny but I was annoyed at myself. I thought why didn't I just say it but—
Q: It's really scary.
A: Yeah, it is. It is. Yeah, I didn't think she was being mean. I think she was actually being—
Q: Trying to get you to—
A: —making a connection or something.
Q: Letting—yeah.
A: And telling me that she knew.
Q: And saying, "It's okay."
A: Yeah. And maybe she was trying to help me, you know thinking why don't you just come out or something but I didn't do it …I think that teachers can be bullied by students and feel threatened, but people don't like to admit that because it makes you seem like you're weak or you're not a good teacher or something. Why would you feel scared of the kids, you know, the students? But people can…Or you're not competent or something or else you'd

be on top of everything and you wouldn't be worried about things like that. Yeah.

Became:

Scene 7: Thick Skin (Dan, Trans Male-Identified Character)

[ANNE plays DAN from inside the circle from 9 to 3. STACY plays the STUDENT seated in a seat in the outer circle at 6.]

Dan: It doesn't help as a teacher
If you don't share things with the class.

Student: *Sir?*

Dan: Because when the kids get to know you better/
They like you better and

Student: *Sir?*

Dan: They respond better.
It makes you a better teacher.
So when you withhold things
You don't get to have a good relationship with them.

We talk a lot about bullying in education these days, and I think
Teachers can be bullied by students
And feel threatened
But teachers don't like to admit it because it makes them seem weak.

Student: *Sir?*

Dan: Or you're not a good teacher
Or you're not competent or you'd be on top of everything.
You wouldn't be worried.

Student: *Sir?*

Dan: Why would you feel scared of the kids, the students?
But you do.

I am happy to be visibly trans
I'm glad that I've been able to do it as a teacher
But it's been extremely difficult.
I don't want it to be this hard for other teachers, younger teachers
I just don't think they could take it. Or SHOULD have to take it.

Student: *Sir?*

Dan: It's taken me many, many years
           and I've developed a very thick skin.

           You need that
           You need a thick skin

Student: *Sir*

Dan: Because the statistics are not good for trans* and gender
           variant peoples' survival.
           Not good at all.

           And education is more conservative than most careers
           So the statistics are even worse.
           Much worse.

Student: *Sir?*

Dan: Oh, I'm surviving. I'm thriving, I am.

Student: *Sir?*

Dan: But I've had to have a very. Thick. Skin.

Transcript Excerpt

And so being in the closet really made me not enjoy the workplace
as much and not feel close to my colleagues, and also made me feel
a little bit like, I wonder if they were, sort of, pitying me 'cause they
must think I don't have much of a life because I don't talk about it very
much. And they never asked why so I thought they must just think, oh,
she lives alone. Not that there's anything wrong with being single but
because people didn't talk to me about anything like that I thought they
must have just written me off as being some kind of—you like people
to know that you've got a good life, that you're happy, that you've got
a partner and a home and things like that. But, yeah, if you can't talk
about them what kind of person are you?

Became:

Scene 8: Oh, She Lives Alone (Fiona, Trans Female-Identified Character)

*[STACY plays FIONA from inside the circle at 12. ANNE plays the
STUDENT circling outside the circle counter-clockwise.]*

Fiona: Being in the closet about both my gender and my sexuality
           Made me not enjoy teaching

I didn't feel close to my colleagues or my students.
Sometimes I felt a little bit like,
I wondered if they were, sort of, pitying me
'Cause they thought I didn't have much of a life
Because I never talked about my personal life.
And they
Never asked.

I thought, they must just think,
Student: *Oh, she lives alone*—not that there's anything wrong with being single
Fiona: But because people didn't talk to me
Didn't ask
About my personal life
I thought, they've just written me off
As being some kind of—
(beat)

You like people to know
You've got a good life/
You're happy/
That you've got a partner
And a home
And things like that.

And, yeah, if you can't share yourself,
Share your life a little bit
Student: *What kind of person are you?*

Transcript Excerpt

But years later when I was at the Pride March—you know the after party sort of thing in the Catani Gardens where everyone sits around I was sitting there with some friends and somebody came up and like poked me in the back or something and I turned around and it was her, it was this kid, who was now probably 20 or something. And so I was right. She was a lesbian 'cause now she was all out and she was at the Pride March. But she didn't have any friends there so she asked if she could sit with our group and I didn't want her to but one of my other friends said, "Yeah." And I was saying, "Oh, can't we get rid of her?" and—This other friend was telling me off saying, "Why are you not

111

being nice to her?" and telling this girl that she should come and join the football club that I was playing for and stuff and I was like, "Shut up." And she did, she came along to football as well but eventually she sort of dropped off 'cause I just refused to talk to her. But she was still doing flirty things. Like we were at the beach and she was trying to push me in the water and things like that, like just constantly playing games with me. And even after I wasn't teaching her any more I just felt like this is not right, not that—you know I didn't like her anyway and I can't remember if I had a girlfriend at the time but I just wasn't interested in her—But she just wouldn't leave me alone. Yeah. And that's veering off the teaching thing but when I was at school I felt very uncomfortable about it and I think that can happen between straight people as well. I know girls have crushes on teachers all the time, like male teachers, and they can get into trouble like that. But it's harder when you're gay because—especially if you're in the closet because you don't know— There' so many more unknowns. I'm not sure what she's doing. I don't even know if she's a lesbian. She doesn't know if I am and I don't know if she thinks I am, and I don't know if any of this is just in my head, or I don't know what's going on. And it's hard to tell anyone about that and make it sound like it's something you should be reporting or something. It's just weird—Yeah. But if you were to say, "I think that girl's got a crush on me and I'm feeling uncomfortable." Or imagine if it was a man, "I think that boy has got a crush on me." And if the parents found out that you'd said that about their kid I'm sure that the blame would be put onto the teacher somehow. Why is he talking about my child—They would think that the teacher was doing it so that's why...

Became:

Scene 10: Blame the Teacher (Pam)

[STACY plays PAM sitting in the centre circle at 12. Anne plays student circling first outside, then inside the circle.]

Pam:	I was at the Pride March—a
	sitting there with some friends—
	And somebody came up and poked me in the back and I turned around and/
Student:	*[pointing] And it was her/*
Pam:	It was that girl, that kid, who was now probably 20 or something.

[beat]
I was right.
Student: *She was queer.*
Pam: She was out and she was at the Pride March.
And she was queer.

She asked if she could sit with our group and
I didn't want her to
But one of my friends said,
Student: *Yeah/*
Pam: And I said NO/

And another friend was telling
this girl she should
Student: *Come and join the football club*
Pam: I was playing for and I was like,
"Shut up."

But she did, she came along to football
[beat]
and I, I just refused to talk to her.
[beat]
I can't remember if I had a girlfriend at the time/
But/
I just wasn't interested in her.
Eventually she stopped coming.
[beat]
I'm not sure what she's doing now.

But that is not a connection—hanging out at pride, playing on
the same footie team—I'm interested in having
With a student/
Even an ex-student, no way.

So it's hard to tell anyone—when that sort of thing happens in
the classroom. Flirting. Crossing boundaries
It's hard to make it sound like it's something/
Student: *Anything/*
Pam: Something you should be reporting.
If you were to say,
"I think that girl's got a crush on me

And I'm feeling uncomfortable" in a professional teaching situation—

And if the parents found out
that you'd
said anything
About their kid,
I'm sure that the blame would be put onto the teacher somehow.

Student: *Why is she talking about my child that way?*
           You should get rid of her –
Pam: They always
Student: *Blame the teacher.*
           Always.

Transcript Excerpt

...it got a point where I wouldn't go shopping after school hours because I would have kids come up to me sometimes in the supermarket, and the kids who I didn't even teach, and give that sort of harassment, and it was really unnerving. Like, I'd never encountered anything like that. And that's why I decided, this isn't worth it. It made me think, initially, I don't want to teach again, but after 20—no, a bit after 25 years. And it also made me re-evaluate where I was living and the lifestyle I was living, and that's what led to me having most of last year off... I was, sort of, outed because I had a property that neighboured another property, obviously, but the father of that, had a son who didn't live there, so he would have learnt very quickly, "Oh, he's gay." So that spread like wildfire... The line the school used was that, "If it's not happening within the school grounds, it's not a school matter."... So to the point where I had teenage boys on motorbikes who—hooning around outside my property, which was, you know, a rural setting. Like, destroying property, I had broken trees and what have you. So I contacted the police, they suggested I contact their parents, and their parents were livid at me, and that fell back on the loophole of, "They're minors, how dare you," and I, sort of, tried to rationalise, "I thought you'd appreciate getting the thumbs up that it could go further if it doesn't stop." So, yeah, there was a real reluctance for the school to act, and certainly for those parents to act.

Became:

Scene 11: Fucking Faggot (Mike, Gay Male-Identified Character)

[ANNE plays MIKE inside the circle, rotating clockwise around the centre group of chairs. STACY plays the STUDENT, seated in the centre circle at 12.]

Mike: I've experienced harassment pretty much my whole career.
And it's ranged in terms of intensity.
On some occasions, I'd hear snide comments like

Student: *He bats for the other team,*
Right through to the really, you know, in-your-face

Student: *You fucking faggot,*

Mike: **That sort of thing.**

I wouldn't go shopping after school hours because I would have kids come up to me in the supermarket,

Student: *He bats for the other team*

Mike: Kids who I didn't even teach,

Student: *You fucking faggot*

Mike: And it was really
[beat]
Unnerving.

Mike: That's what made me think I didn't want to teach anymore, after 20 no, after 25 years.
That's what led to me having a year off, on stress leave and also moving back to the city.

See, when I was teaching at a middle school out there
In the country
I was, sort of,
No. I was outed, by a student.

Because I had a property that neighboured one of my students' property.

Student: *Look at him! The fucking faggot.*

Mike: And he outed me.
It spread amongst the other boys like wildfire.
Spread it into my private environment, my home life
[beat]

There were a number of ugly incidents on my property
Teenage boys on motorbikes
Hooning around outside my home/

Student: *Fucking faggot/*

Mike: Destroying property/
Breaking trees, breaking fences/

Student: *You fucking faggot.*

Mike: The line the school used was,

Student: *If it's not happening within the school grounds*
It's not a school matter.

Mike: So I contacted the police, but they only suggested I/

Student: *Contact the kids' parents/*

Mike: Which I did.

The parents were livid, fell back on the whole

Student: *They're minors, just kids, how dare you.*

Mike: Like it was **my** fault

Student: *How dare/*

Mike: Like it was up to me/

Student: *You/*

Mike: They blamed me/

Student: *Fucking faggot.*
[beat]

Mike: So yeah, I took some time off.

Transcript Excerpt

I think that there's this sort of attitude amongst the administration as well at the school that they've sort of been benevolent to support this process, and so I should just shut up and—because I'm fairly vocal about everything at work, not just about gender and sexuality. So it's sort of this—I don't know. I had an odd conversation with one of my APs on the last day of term, where he sort of noticed that I had some facial hair growing and was sort of gently mocking that, and was asking how're the kids dealing with it and, "Oh, they call you sir, that's fantastic." And I was like, ugh. It's just this really sort of strange idea that if people recognise my male identity, then they are doing me this big favour, I guess, and the school's doing me—

Q: You should be grateful and—

A: —doing me this big favour.

… I came out to all staff in a staff meeting this year… It was like 140—it was actually really good. It was like—there's 140 staff at the school, teaching and non-teaching staff. So there's like a core of people that I'm friends with outside of school who I had known for a long time in one way or another, if not consciously. So I had them—and it also just felt like a way to take the power away from the people who were going to be mean, so like if I'm standing up in a staff meeting saying, "I'm trans, this is the language you need to use," ta-da-da, it sort of took their power away. Because if they weren't going to respect my gender identity they were at least going to respect the fact that I could do that. But, yeah, like a couple of staff members walked out of that presentation, and admin didn't pick them up on it. The—the staff members said it was for personal reasons, and so therefore that was okay. And that was sort of the first warning sign that like this isn't—capital S support doesn't really mean anything if they are not willing to—Yeah. So I came out to all my classes this year, because I started taking testosterone last holidays, so my voice is starting to change, and I'm starting to grow some facial hair, some ridiculous facial hair and things, so I was going to come out to the students practically even if I didn't want to. But, I mean, I was never worried about their reaction. I've never, I mean, you have one or two incidents. I'm sure they talk about it, but they overwhelmingly—I gave them permission to ask questions as long as they were respectful and that kind of thing. And it's been fantastic. Like the kids—Yeah. And then I came out to the Year 10s as well, and in the assembly. The first assembly for the year. It was pretty—I mean, I know those kids really well because I've been the year coordinator for a year, so I like to think that—I mean, I'm sure some of them hate me, but I've got a pretty good relationship with them, and it wasn't—I wasn't—I was way more scared of the staff meeting than I was of the kids. And especially because I knew if I gave them permission to ask questions that were respectful, that they would use that well—like I trusted them enough to do that. Oh, they asked some really funny questions, but, yeah, nothing offensive or disrespectful, or—And they've been fantastic. I mean, they all call me Mr Smith and use male pronouns, and even if they slip up, they're not— they're not bad about, like—when staff members slip up, they tend to be really like make it, it's all about them. It's all about, "I'm so sorry, I'm trying, it's just so hard," that kind of thing. Whereas with kids, they're like, "Sorry," "Oh, all right." And just, let's move on. So that's been, yeah, it's been really, really good with the kids. They've been fantastic. And they actually apparently had a Facebook—this is a nice story which made me feel happy. They all put up like some Facebook status in support of me, apparently—it was going around the school, so it was really nice, and a little bit heart warming, only, yeah, because I was feeling quite insecure about the staff reaction, and probably parent reaction…

Became:

Scene 13: They Call Me Sir (Dan)

[ANNE plays DAN in the centre circle at 3. STACY stands next to DAN—too close—as MR HALL.]

Dan: So it's sort of—I don't know.
            I basically took up my position here as a lesbian, as an out lesbian, and they were pretty supportive. I stayed like that for a few years, sort of testing the waters. But in my fourth year, I went ahead and started to transition. I started taking T over the break, and I knew it would make some pretty visible pretty rapid changes.
            The school was sort of less supportive then.
            There were issues about which toilet I could use, stuff like that.
            I came out as male at a staff meeting, and some of the older staff actually stood up and walked out. They were just over it. Queer fatigue.
            So yeah.
            But I kept going, I felt I had to do this, and that a job shouldn't stop me. The kids were fine. Totally flexible. No judgment, some respectful questions, that's about it.
            But the staff? Not so much.
            I had an odd conversation
            With one of my Assistant Principals—David, Mr Hall—on the last day of term. Just after the assembly—I do the sound system—
            Where he noticed that I had some facial hair growing/

Mr Hall: *What's that—is that? [flicks face]. Is that HAIR?/*

Dan: Some facial hair, and was sort of gently mocking/

Mr Hall: *What's that – you've got something on your face there—*
            [flicks face]—is s that a bit of HAIR?/

Dan: And he was asking how're the **kids** dealing with it and,
            I said—
            "Yeah, it's going well, they call me sir for the most part
            now"/

Mr Hall: *Sir? Do you have a girlfriend sir?*

Dan: And he was like:

Mr Hall: (chorus) *Oh, they call you sir, that's fantastic.*
            [beat]

Dan: And I was like/
            UGH.
            It's just
            It's just this strange idea that if people recognise my male
            identity, then they are doing me this big favour, I guess, the
            school's doing me

Mr Hall: *"Oh, they call you sir, that's fantastic."*

Dan: *[beat]*
            I must admit
            I often think about leaving my workplace
            And choosing another school.
            Part of me doesn't want to until I can fully pass
            And be confident in passing, like, close to 100% of the time

Mr Hall: *100% percent*

Dan: Because it would be a lot easier.

            But then I think, well, if I go
            And I'm just a male teacher, what is that?

Mr Hall: *Sir?*

Dan: Really, what IS that?
            [beat]
            It would be a lot easier but. What kind of person would I be?

            I'm always going to be the trans teacher here,
            Which has pros and cons in terms of what
            I feel like I could do for kids.

            So if I go to another school
            And I'm there as male then—like that's just going to

Mr Hall: *Sir?/*
Dan: It would be so bizarre/
Mr Hall: *What kind of/*
Dan: To be in a school environment as a—read as—male.
Mr Hall: *Person are you?/*
Dan: Another
Mr Hall: *White male teacher in a secondary school!*

Dan: What is THAT?
           If I had just gone in as an Anglo male.
           There's kids that I wouldn't have worked with
           that wouldn't have had that confidence
           To make themselves known to me
           Unless I outed myself.
           So yeah. They call me sir. And it's fantastic.

AUDIENCE FEEDBACK ON THE WORKSHOP PERFORMANCE OF *OUT/IN FRONT*

The audience was overwhelmingly positive about the performance. One audience member who identified as a gay female secondary teacher was very emotional, wanting to share how meaningful it was to her to see 'herself' portrayed onstage. As queer teachers (and researchers and artists), we are familiar with emotional response. So while the workshop performance created it an amazing feeling of solidarity and sense that we were—together—doing politically important work—it was also personally healing to be able to tell these stories and embody them in ways that page-based research just can't do or do in the same fulsome way.

The most positive feedback centred on the element of 'fun' and 'play' in the performance, but audience members were also clear that this play also carried with it risk. The audience wondered how we might replicate the performance on proscenium stage with a more general audience, and so did we. There was much productive dialogue about ways to stage the performance to retain the important balance of play and risk. Most importantly, the dialogue centred on our commitment to portraying the experience of the queer teachers who had been interviewed, who almost all narrated the stress of feeling that they were being 'watched', constantly 'visible', and not fully able to share themselves (or their lives) as teachers or people in their workplaces. The most challenging aspect of transitioning this workshop performance to a full-length production for a proscenium stage and a general audience was then was to make a piece of theatre in which the queer teachers were the 'centre stage' being 'watched' by outside others—audience members who were let off the hook as non-queer teachers never can be in schools (Harris & Farrington, 2014).

REHEARSING/DEVISING AND...

In this chapter, we've explored the rehearsing and devising process we used to develop the script for *Out/In Front* for the Singapore performance. The next chapter details some of the revising and performing process we took up as we moved from this text-based workshop toward a fully produced production that took on the challenge of making the audience 'accountable' to/in the stories of queer teachers.

REVISING/PERFORMING

WE'RE GOING TO FEAST FESTIVAL!

In Chapter Six we detailed how we adapted research transcripts into the script *Out/In Front* and discussed the devised workshop performance that Anne and Stacy performed at the International Drama in Education Research Institute Conference in Singapore. In this chapter, we detail some of our devising process as we moved from this workshop performance for the full professional festival production of *Heavier Than Air* as part of the Feast Festival in Adelaide, Australia, in November 2015. Part of this work involved adapting the performance from in-the-round staging. Because staging is inexorably tied to the content and politic of the work and because the area staging worked so effectively in the workshop performance, we had our work cut out for us because we still wanted to retain the impact of implicating the audience in the stories of queer teachers and their workplace issues. The development process raised questions about how devised work—and how performance work devised from interviews—constitutes ethnodrama, or otherwise conceived verbatim theatre and further how we might otherwise consider the power of embodied performance drawn from 'data'.

This chapter features the script *Heavier Than Air* as it was performed at the Feast Festival. The playscript included eight characters (four male-identified characters played by Anne and four female-identified played by Rachel Forgasz). The show was performed twice; just before the second show, the performers, four queer teachers, and one member of the South Australia Safe Schools Coalition participated in a pre-show forum. While the protections and safeguards for LGBTIQ students in Australia are growing, there are few such protections for queer teachers. This show maintained its overtly political agenda as we sought to raise awareness of workplace health and safety issues for LGBTIQ teachers, and to advance a conversation within the education sector and more widely about how schools might better support their queer teachers and make schools less treacherous workplaces.

Feedback from the original research participants, audience members, queer teachers, and school principals and other administrators was again overwhelmingly positive. We learned that the experience of queer teachers in schools is a topic that needs discussing and the public performance of interview transcripts is a powerful way to explore it together. The idea that performance is a powerful mode and medium for such public discussions is not new; however, we need more discussion of the challenges and considerations writers, performers, and directors encounter when working to make research and interview source material into a compelling, stand-on-its own performance text. So here, to begin, are some of the key issues and questions that emerged from the Singapore workshop performance. We used these issues and questions as we embarked on a four-month devising and performance process. Throughout this period, we worked with deviser and performance ethnography scholar Christine Sinclair and performer Rachel Forgasz. Following a discussion of our revising process, we include the performance playscript. However, keep in mind that this is not a 'final' script in any sense, but rather the script we settled on for the Feast Festival performance in November 2015.

REVISING

Based on the feedback and audience discussion in Singapore, four major themes/issues required rewriting/revising/addressing. Below we discuss each theme and how we resolved the issue for the Feast Festival production. While these themes are not unusual, we want to stress that rewriting and re-devising is always context-specific for each new performance (even of fully scripted plays), and always tied to considerations of casting, venue, and production contexts.

Audience Involvement

Our first consideration was how to maintain the audience interaction in the performance. However, we were aware that our Singapore audience was probably the most reliable and sympathetic audience we would get. Like all performers, we didn't want to risk including elements that required audience participation and find that the audience did not want to participate! At the same time, knowing that we were heading to a queer arts and culture festival meant that we would be 'preaching to the converted' and we did not want to state (or perform) the obvious. So the games that we had originally (and very spontaneously!) devised for the Singapore performance were both gimmicky in some ways, and risky: we all object to being alienated by defensive or 'too clever' performers who end up putting the audience off centre in their efforts to make an 'impact'. For example, we were most worried about the game in which we left the 'most straight' audience members uncomfortably standing outside the playing circle, which seemed to alienate some of them; at the same time, this was a favourite game of other audience members.

For Feast Festival, we knew that the potential audience size meant we could not count on getting everyone onto the stage of interacting in such an activity, but we still wanted them to be 'implicated' in the performance. After lots of experimenting with words, movement, games, and us playing from the audience, we found that we could create that still included the audience at times in the role of 'the class', without calling them up on stage or risking offending anyone.

In the final script for Feast Festival, we settled on four games that both actors played with the audience. The games involved paper in some way (games with fortune tellers or 'chatterboxes'—remember those?—and paper airplanes), and were less 'confronting' versions of our original games from Singapore. Still, the games asked people to examine their own practices in schools and gender/sexuality, and provided opportunities for them to interact with the stage/actors, but from their seats. It was a compromise, but one that we could live with and still retain the ethos of the original performance.

Agit Prop Elements and Performance Style

Thinking about audience involvement also helped us develop an overall performance aesthetic or style for *Heavier Than Air*. We began with a comment from one participant, Helen, who had been scribbling on one of the pieces of paper on the chairs, left to keep the seat free for us as we performed. As we noted in Chapter Six, Helen loved the paper's tactile qualities and wanted to be more involved in using and working with the paper—folding it writing on it, making things with it. It reminded her of being in class and paper being everywhere and the possibilities (and oppression) of paper in schools.

We took her provocation and eventually Stacy devised a sequence of poems and activities and images around the notion of paper. In our rehearsals, we played with the idea of a paper shredder, piles of paper building up in classrooms, teachers drowning in stacks of paper, audience members passing notes. And while in the end we did not use the shredder or the bulk of the 'volume' devising experiments, they all informed the development of the script. The poems stayed in as 'interludes' and we used paper folding and origami as the central activity and design element of the performance. We worked with the ideas of paper as a skin between us and the world and paper as both a 'tool' of transformation and also a 'tool' that oppresses—a weapon of homophobia and transphobia on which gossipy notes, displinary letters home, and letters of resignation are written; on which both violent and imaginative pictures are drawn. In the final version of the script, paper became the central metaphor of queer teachers in school, and the title changed to *Heavier than Air*, a reference to how queer teachers, like airplanes, are able to achieve 'heavier than air flight', despite the weight of harassment, bullying, and homo/transphobia they experience in the lives as teachers and at school.

In addition, we created a series of PowerPoint slides that served two functions. First, the slides marked the three sections of the play through origami diagrams that move from the 'common operations' of simple folds like a mountain fold, to folds that involve more manipulation of the paper like rotating and pleating, to folds that transform the paper into an object with a life and liveliness of its own, like the paper airplane. These three sections—common operations; rotate, pleat, repeat; and flight—echo and parallel the increasingly complex and challenging stories and characters in the play. Second, the origami diagrams on the slides served a practical function, demonstrating the steps for folding that the actors on stage were taking the audience through in the folding games in the performance.

Finally, we included a brief sound effects track that included the sounds of a school bell ringing and children on a playground. These sound effects marked the transition between scenes in the performance.

Figure 8. Heavier Than *Air title slide. Photo by A.B.*

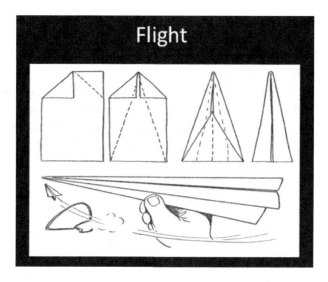

Figure 9. Flight Slide

Diversity of Characters

After about eight weeks of rehearsing and improvising with Rachel and Anne, we decided on the characters that resonated the most with us, and Anne shaped the script and combined some of the characters to both represent the broadest possible range of experiences and in order to make some coherent through-lines and a 'story' with a build. The character of Dan emerged as the protagonist, and his interactions with Mr Hall, his boss, and his co-workers also made him a central figure—as many of the other teachers talked primarily about their students. Dan's story of beginning work at his first school as an out lesbian and then transitioning to male-identified was also a rather remarkable story that audiences really connected with. Around him we arranged a cast of six characters who all portrayed an aspect of the broad range of queer teacher experiences, from wonderful and fulfilling, to challenging and painful.

Some scholars have been very interested in the degree to which a script like *Heavier Than Air* are verbatim—that is, a script comprised of word-for-word excerpts from interview transcripts, with no additions or reworking. We estimate that this script is approximately 85% the teachers' own words. But we also point out that we are all (or have been) queer teachers, and our own experiences have also shaped the script and performance, whether 'verbatim' or not. In addition, as a work of art, we encourage playwrights

127

and devisers to pursue what is right for your artwork, and not be rigidly constrained by categories that may fall short of what your performance is telling you it wants or needs to be or do. Scholarly definitions and discourses are there to help us make sense of the world, not limit it, and for this reason we do not identify this piece as explicitly a piece of verbatim theatre, forum theatre, or ethnodrama. It is, instead, a devised playscript about the experiences of queer teachers in schools based on and informed by interviews with actual queer teachers.

Non-Didactic Theatre from Research Interviews

In a related way, the play offers readers an example of the complex work of adapting interview data into a work of art. While of course there is a long and well-documented type of theatre called 'didactic theatre'—work that seeks to educate audiences—we are hoping our example goes beyond suggesting ways to make instructional theatre. As we have tried to highlight above, categorical understandings of any work of art are only a place to begin, not end, in a relationship with a piece of work. So one of the real challenges of working with interview data is to make a piece of work that stands on its own and tells a story as a play, and this is why we were so pleased to be able to bring the piece to the Feast Festival. Our third performance opportunity is upcoming in January 2017, when we return to Singapore where it started, and perform the play again in the Singapore Fringe Festival. This time, it will be a public theatrical performance that is not targeted at/for queer audiences. So once again (and perhaps more so) we will test the work's ability to reach audiences, highlighting once again the context-specific nature of all theatre.

When we were devising the play, we changed the words of the interviews only when the words as spoken got in the way of our ability to reach the audience. While enhancing these words with embodiments that may or may not have been very different from those of the people who originally spoke those words in interview, and using some stylized movements to highlight some of the dialogue, we felt our commitment to the words themselves—and to the lived experiences of these teachers—needed to be focused on their overall impact, rather than the verbatim lines. Whether you feel you must shape a performance to the interviews or other 'data' being used in your writing, or vice versa, we encourage you above all to remain committed to a final product that effectively and artfully conveys your core meaning or message.

PERFORMING *HEAVIER THAN AIR*

The following script is the 'formal' playscript we used in the Feast Festival performance. As we note above, we consider this script the second stage of creative development of the work.

CAST/CHARACTERS

(Anne)
Dan, trans, male-identified
Mike, gay male-identified
Ben, gay male-identified

(Rachel)
Kaz, queer female-identified
Fiona, older trans, female-identified lesbian
Pam, pansexual, female-identified

PP SLIDE 1: IMAGE OF PAPER AIRPLANE

SFX: PLAYGROUND 30 SECONDS

[ANNE and RACHEL Play 'chatterboxes' with the audience as they enter, all questions/statements based on gender and sexuality.]

SFX: PLAYGROUND—BELL 26 SECONDS

PP SLIDE 2: HEAVIER THAN AIR

Prologue

[DAN sets up the microphone for Mr Hall.]

Mr Hall, Principal: Can you hear me?

Dan, the Teacher: Yes, Sir.

Mr Hall: Can you hear me, hello?

Dan: Yes we can hear you. Sir—the mic is on.

Mr Hall: Okay, great. So if it gets fuzzy, just let me know, okay?

Dan: Sure, yes. Mr Hall, you're on. You are live. I mean, the microphone is live.
[taps the microphone]

Mr Hall: Ok, good. Are you ready? Helllllo?

Dan: SIR! I said yes. I just said – the mic is—

Mr Hall: Ladies and gentlemen, good morning! Welcome to Day One. We believe that schooling should be enjoyable for both students AND teachers, and that every student and teacher matters. This year we have many new teachers with us. And how lucky are YOU? Our school is acclaimed as a great school. Not only by reputation, but because of YOU, our outstanding teachers. We choose our teachers carefully. Ladies and gentlemen, welcome to the new school year.

[beat]

Thank you Dan, you can turn the microphone off now.

SFX: BELL_SOLO for 5 SECONDS

PP SLIDE 3: COMMON OPERATIONS

Scene 1: Thick Skin (Dan)

[DAN passes out TOO MUCH paper to the audience, then comes onstage. He begins the first origami move by instructing audience in mountain fold/ valley fold. RACHEL folds along like a student, whose lines are indicated in italics. Shared lines are indicated in bold.]

It doesn't help as a teacher
If you don't share things with the class.
Sir?
Because when the kids get to know you better/
They like you better and
Sir?
They respond better.
It makes you a better teacher.
So when you withhold things
You don't get to have a good relationship with them.

We talk a lot about bullying in education these days, and I think
Teachers can be bullied by students
And feel threatened
But teachers don't like to admit it because it makes them seem weak.
Sir?
Or you're not a good teacher
Or you're not competent or you'd be on top of everything.

You wouldn't be worried.
Sir?
Why should you feel scared of the kids, the students?
But you do.

I am happy to be visibly trans
I'm glad that I've been able to do it as a teacher
But it's been extremely difficult.
I don't want it to be this hard for other teachers, younger teachers
I just don't think they could take it. Or SHOULD have to take it.
Sir?
It's taken me many, many years
and I've developed a very thick skin.

You need that
You need a thick skin
Because the stats are not good for trans* and gender variant peoples' survival,
Not good at all.

And education is more conservative than most careers
So the stats are even worse./
Much worse.//
Sir?
Oh, I'm surviving. I'm thriving, I am.
Sir?
But I've had to have a very. Thick. Skin.

[DAN asks audience to pass their papers down to the end, sits on stool. Rachel collects the papers and becomes KAZ.]

Scene 2: Really Really Short Hair (Kaz)

[ANNE plays the student, whose lines are indicated in italics.]

I've always had really short hair, really quite short hair/
Do you have a boyfriend Miss?"

it's really hard for me to hide my sexuality, see./
Why do you have short hair?
well, it's funny like/*Miss—*
when I knew I was going to become a teacher/
Miss do you have kids?
Twelve months before I started my Dip Ed
I started growing my hair longer

131

So I could fly under the radar and not have to/
Miss—what's your boyfriend's name?
Deal with homophobia
And try to get a job at the same time.

So my hair **was** pretty short.
Miss, do you have a partner?
I grew it long, sort of to about there-ish, but I was just
so queer!
Miss—
Blind Freddy would have seen it./
"Miss, do you have kids?" "How old are you Miss? Do you have a partner?
Do you have a boyfriend Miss?"/

And the very first week at work a student says,
Miss, why do you have short hair?
And I said, "Why do **you** have short hair?"

They're trying to work out the social codes.

Miss, do you have kids?
Trying to work out what means what
And how it relates to them.
Still. It doesn't stop them.
From going too far.

The latest form of harassment
Has been the Year Sevens saying to me in class openly:
"How old are you Miss, why don't you have kids? Do you have a partner?
Do you have a boyfriend Miss?"

That's the constant. Just last week, a girl constantly saying:
"Do you have a boyfriend, what's your boyfriend's name?"

And I, I just ignored it. Tried to redirect. Tried to move on.
And she—she just kept asking.
"Do you have a boyfriend, what's your boyfriend's name?"
Would not/
"Do you have a boyfriend?
Stop.
"What's your boyfriend's name?"

In the end I said,
Emily. you will have to stop. Because that. is sexual. harassment.

(in wonder) And she did…!
[beat]
(slowly building) *"Oh Miss,*
"You look like Ellen. She has short hair, just like you. Miss, do you know
Ellen miss?"

SFX: BELL_SOLO

RACHEL DOES STAND UP GAME #1: STAY STANDING

Everyone stand up.

Stay standing if you have a name that could belong to a person of either gender.

Stay standing if you've ever been mistaken as someone of another gender.

Choose one audience member still standing, play chatter boxgame.

RACHEL'S ANSWER TO CHATTERBOX GAME: You can sit down.

SFX: BELL_SOLO

Scene 3: 100% Present (Mike)

[MIKE delivers monologue within the small square of space between stools.
KAZ is sitting on the floor, cutting a paper skirt.]

I think it comes down to location, demographics, what kids are exposed to.
—those things influence your experience as a teacher.
I was teaching in St. Kilda, for example, in what was certainly not an affluent school—
But they're exposed to a lot of things, a lot more than kids in the country maybe.
To those kids, gayness is just not an issue—and I'm not saying that they're all pro-gay rights, not at all.
But they can articulate what they think and what they feel
Can see both sides much better.

Because of **location**
And **demographics**
And what they're **exposed to.**

It's taken a long time
15-plus years
To come to terms with my own sexuality.

Its great to now feel so comfortable
Within myself
And with myself
At school.

[MIKE rolls out a paper 'red carpet' from upstage centre, then:]

But I would still say you're never a 100% present
As a gay teacher, I'm never 100% present in the room
The way others are able to be
Never 100% there, as a teacher, as a person.
As a gay man.
Never. 100% there.

Scene 4: To Be Honest (Kaz)

[KAZ puts on paper skirt and walks down the 'runway' while speaking. ANNE its on stool and plays the student while making a paper fan.]

I wear lots of skirts
Dresses. Femme stuff.
I do that very consciously.

And I ask my students, when there's an opportunity
Miss do you have a boyfriend?
A teachable moment,
"How can you tell if someone is gay?"
And the kids will go/
—By the way they look.
And I'm like, "Okay, so…I must be" ?? *[points to her skirt]*
Oh yeah [realisation]
I incorporate that, and I use that gender stereotype
(out) *Oh yeah, yeah*
That femme stereotype
(out) The way you look…!
To challenge the gay story line.

So I wear skirts, dresses.
A very conscious thing.
I think it makes me a little bit less intimidating, to the kids
I'm being stereotypical, of course.

But another teacher? She copped a lot of homophobia from kids because, well,

She looked really butch.
She looked really butch. So.

I mean, schools are such gendered places.
The school uniform alone is so gendered.
Presenting anything outside of that,
whether you're a student or a teacher
you just cop that attention and it's often negative.
So?
So.

[beat]
To be quite honest?
I kind of wish I had the guts to be a bit more butch
Really butch [ANNE'S is a question]
but I feel like that would be, almost,
counterproductive.
[beat]
To be honest.

[Kaz gathers up paper and pushes it downstage.]

SFX: PLAYGROUND_30 SECONDS

PP SLIDE 4: MOUNTAIN AND VALLEY

Interlude I: Folding (Dan)

[DAN has a huge, oversized chatterbox and is playing with it while he speaks this interlude; downstage centre; RACHEL plays a student, following along with her own smaller chatterbox, upstage.]

You and I
are born from folding.
Changing from one form
into another

Transforming something
making it smaller,
pushing pulling rotating.

Not adding.
Not subtracting.
Just valley and mountain.

Mountain and Valley.
[beat]

PP SLIDE 5: ROTATE, PLEAT, REPEAT

Scene 5: You Know the Statistics (Fiona)

[RACHEL upstage on floor; ANNE upstage facing wall, then moves to stool and plays student as monologue unfolds.]

I used to be Mr Buck.
When I started teaching I was a heterosexual male/
Married to a woman/
To my wife Jennifer.
[stands.]

Eventually, along the way
I came out as female
Changed my name to Fiona
Began living as a woman. At work and at home.

I was still married to Jennifer
And we were
We appeared to be
Lesbians.
It was a long, slow process
My transition.

For a while I didn't like to identify as anything.
Anything.
I didn't have words for it.
It's hard in a school/
To not have words for what you are
And it's hard in a relationship too.
It was a difficult time.

Before that
Before my transition
I had an opportunity,
a good opportunity
To come out in a class once
And I didn't do it.
I think the student who was talking

Must've been a lesbian, I suppose.
Must've been.

There were about 19, 20 kids in the room *[ANNE to stool]*
And we were just sitting around and she said,
"You know, the statistics say that two in every 20 people are gay/
And there's 20 people in this room."
And then she just looked at me [laughs] and I was like, "Yeah, that is true."

She was like, *"I wonder who they are."*
She just stared at me. And I stared back. I couldn't do it.
I just couldn't do it.
I'd gotten so used to dodging questions and I just – yeah.
I was annoyed at myself. I thought, why didn't I
Just say it?

I didn't think she was being mean.
I think she was actually being
Trying to make a connection, actually.
Telling me that **she saw me.**

[out] And maybe she was trying to help me, you know,
thinking
Why don't you just come out?
And so she asked./She asked and she waited.//
But I didn't do it.
I just couldn't do it. I just couldn't do it.

SFX: PLAYGROUND_BELL_26 SECONDS

Scene 6: I Chose My School Carefully (Ben)

[BEN rolls out paper and draws a primary school rainbow down on floor.
RACHEL helps as a primary student.]

I want to note
For the record please?
I want to note that as a gay teacher
I knew I would be judged before I even started.

As a gay teacher you have to be very intentional/
And that starts with choosing where you will work—if you have that luxury—
because sometimes you just need a job.

So I chose my school carefully.
I'm not aware of any policies that protect queer teachers
But at MY school it's just not an issue.
Diversity here is just normal, you know?
That might sound weird, like 'diversity is normal'
So then what's diverse about it?
But yeah.
There's a general acceptance of diversity.

Our thing is that we embrace everybody and that we embrace difference
And we embrace creativity
So creative children who, in other mainstream schools might be singled out
As being different, in this school we're all just—
Normal.
Everything's accepted.
That's why I chose my school carefully.
[beat]
[stands]
The underlying policy in my classroom is respect
And that's respect in all its forms:
Kids respecting each other/
And them respecting me/
And me respecting them/
And part of that is my belief that
It's okay to be gay.

And to communicate that to kids effectively
You have to be okay with it yourself/
You have to be okay … with yourself/
You can't say, "It's okay to be different,"
But then you hide this aspect of yourself/

I was wearing a pink jumper
And the kids asked me, *Why are you wearing pink?*
and I said, "I really like the colour pink," and some of the boys were like,
"*I like pink*"

They were willing to say it,
I like pink
because I'm willing to say it. I like pink, too.
They're willing to think that they don't have to be

Boy-boys.
They can be whoever they want to be.
So if they want to play house
Or they want to play cooking
Or wear pink
I encourage it.
[beat]

This is why I chose my school carefully.
I would love every school to be like my school.
It would be fantastic for all children to be able to experience
That kind of diversity. That kind of education.

If every school,
If every school was my school, it would be great.

[ANNE and RACHEL begin gathering paper up.]

SFX: PLAYGROUND_BELL_26 SECODS (BELL FOR 5 SECONDS ONLY)

PP SLIDE 6: REVERSE FOLD

ANNE & RACHEL DO STAND UP GAME #2: HOW COMFORTABLE ARE YOU?

[All seats in audience have a sachet of rainbow coloured paper under them. ANNE and RACHEL instruct the audience members to find those papers and pick a colour response to the question, "How comfortable are you with talking about your home life at work?"]

ANNE and RACHEL suggest responses:

Red: Not at all/STOP/don't go there, etc.

Yellow: It depends, sometimes, maybe, etc.

Green: All the time, perfectly comfortable, I'm an open book, etc.

[ANNE AND RACHEL instruct the audience to choose a colour response, crumple the paper into a ball, and throw it onto the stage, so at the end there is a rainbow of coloured paper on the stage, which we then 'analyse' as coloured data.]

Rachel: Let us just analyse this data for a few minutes...*[she sweeps the balls thrown stage right]*.

Scene 7: I Didn't Say Anything/Tuning the Ukeles (Pam and Ben)

[PAM sweeps the balls/BEN sits on the floor, organising the. PAM tries unsuccessfully to get his attention.]

Pam: So there was an incident
Where I think a girl was/
Flirting with me in class.

Ben: Listen: How I have survived, how I have made myself at home in my school
is by focusing on the students but also the wider community.

Pam: She was a year 10 student, so probably about 15, 16 years old.
And she would come up/
And sit on my desk/
And ask me personal questions.
And she would
She would do things.

Ben: What I would say to you is this: Choose your school carefully. Pay attention to
the location, the demographics of the school.
MY school is a primary school, a rainbow school. Everything is integrated.
It's all interconnected.

Pam: I remember her grabbing my pencil case once.
She grabbed it and I said
Give it back,
And she was all like,
No.

Like she wanted me to, sort of, chase her.
She was just too interested and,
Playing games with me all the time.

Ben: That is such a secondary school issue.
I said to one of the year 2 kids the other day
I said, "Oh hi Ant,"
I said, "Can you tell your mum thanks for tuning all those ukuleles in the classroom?"
And Ant's little friend goes. *[out]* "He's got two mums. Which mum tuned the ukeleles?"
So it's like that.

Integrated. Interconnected.

Pam: And I felt uncomfortable because I thought,
She's queer
And maybe she knows that
I'm queer *[ANNE: She's queer]*
And I felt like
she's crossing over boundaries and I didn't—
Didn't want her to

Ben: I don't think my experience is the norm.
I don't believe I would experience this in other schools
[beat]
Maybe I've just been lucky.

Pam: But I wasn't sure what to do about it
'Cause she hadn't done anything –

Anything I could tell somebody else to make them believe me.
And it might sound like I'm thinking of *her* in a sexual way
If I said something/
Said anything/
So I didn't.
I just let it go.

Ben: But what did you DO?
Pam: I waited for the school year to be over/
And I just let it go.
I didn't say anything.

Ben: I guess I've just been lucky.

[BEN sweeps paper balls and moves upstage…PAM continues.]

Scene 8: Blame the Teacher (Pam)

[ANNE plays the student upstage to the right of PAM.]

A few years later, I was at the Pride March –
sitting there with some friends –
And somebody came up and poked me in the back and I turned around and/
And it was her/
It was that girl, that kid, who was now probably 20 or something.
[beat]

I was right.
She was queer.
She was out and she was at the Pride March.
And she was queer.

She asked if she could sit with our group and
I didn't want her to
But one of my friends said, Yeah/
And I said NO/

And another friend was telling
this girl she should
Come and join the football club
I was playing for and I was like,
"Shut up."

But she did, she came along to football
[beat]
and I, I just refused to talk to her.
[beat]
I can't remember if I had a girlfriend at the time/
But/
I just wasn't interested in her.
Eventually she stopped coming.
[beat]
I'm not sure what she's doing now.

[ANNE crosses downstage to the left, stopping half-way.]

But that is not a connection I want to make—hanging out at pride, playing on
the same footie team—Not with a student/
Even an **ex-student**, no way.

So it's hard to tell anyone—when that sort of thing happens in the classroom.
Flirting. Crossing boundaries
It's hard to make it sound like it's something/
Anything/
Something you should be reporting.
If you were to say,
**"I think that girl's got a crush on me
And I'm feeling uncomfortable"** in a professional teaching situation—

And if the parents found out

that you'd
said anything
About their kid,
I'm sure that the blame would be put onto the teacher somehow.
Why is she talking about my child that way?
You should get rid of her –
They always
Blame the teacher.
Always.
[beat]

SFX: BELL_SOLO

PP SLIDE 7: FLIGHT

ANNE DOES STAND UP GAME # 3: PAPER AIRPLANE (Dan)

[DAN teaches the audience to fold a paper airplane. Instructs audience to not fly the planes, but to hold them until recess].

SFX: BELL_SOLO

Scene 9: Oh She Lives Alone (Fiona)

[ANNE sits on stool, plays student who cuts a string of paper dolls.]

Being in the closet about both my gender and my sexuality
Made me not enjoy teaching
I didn't feel close to my colleagues or my students.
Sometimes I felt a little bit like,
I wondered if they were, sort of, pitying me
'Cause they thought I didn't have much of a life
Because I never talked about my personal life.
And they
Never asked.

I thought, they must just think,
Oh, she lives alone—not that there's anything wrong with being single
But because people didn't talk to me
Didn't ask
About my personal life
I thought, they've just written me off
As being some kind of—
[beat]

You like people to know
You've got a good life/
You're happy/
That you've got a partner
And a home
And things like that.
So, yeah, if you can't share yourself,
Share your life a little bit
[ANNE holds up string of paper dolls]: What kind of person are you?
What kind of person are you?

SFX: PLAYGROUND_BELL 26 SECONDS

PP SLIDE 8: GENERATING LIFT

Interlude IV: Heavier Than Air (Dan)

[DAN delivers in spoken word style; RACHEL makes paper airplane.]

Paper airplanes.
Models for pushing
some things down—
blame, the accumulation of aggressions,
queer fatigue—
While lifting other things up—
respect, recognition, confidence.
Making space
for heaver-than-air flight.

The application of power
to the resistance
of air.
Generating lift,
making yourself known.
Folding the laws of nature
the dignity of life,
the expression of affection
into
and out of your work—
into and out of this heavier than air work

*[ANNE drops paper; RACHEL flies airplane into the audience from centre
stage.]*

Scene 10: Miss Mason Actually Is a Lez (Kaz)

[DAN exits; ANNE walks around to sit on RACHEL'S stool as the student and school administrator.]

I went to the school musical with my partner
We were in line and I heard/
Hi Miss.
I turned around and it was a girl I didn't know, and she smiled and said hello.
I was a bit sceptical, you know, Why are you saying hello to me?
Hi Miss. Do you have a boyfriend Miss? [giggles]
And then my partner said, "I think she just took a photo of us."
So I turned around again
Hi Miss.
And she smiled. Again. And it was all a bit secretive
Hard to know what had happened.

The next day a year seven came up to me,
showed me a Facebook post of that photo of us with the statement "**Miss Mason actually IS a lez.**"
Hi Miss.
And that went viral by the end of that day.

[ANNE becomes school administrator and turns pages in the manual.]

Straight teachers don't realise
How out they are about their sexuality/
Every time they talk about their spouses
It's just part of –
They don't even question it.
Whereas if you're like me
You're constantly thinking about the words you're choosing.
It's exhausting./
So one of the first questions
I always ask on a school job interview
Is to have a look at the staff handbook
To see if homophobia is covered.
And I'm always disappointed.

In my first school I asked the welfare officer
Is homophobia covered?
Knowing it wasn't in there, in the staff handbook

And she said.
Oh, yeah, well you just assume. You just assume that it's covered.
Even though it's not really covered./

[ANNE crosses to RACHEL'S stool, returns to being the student.]

And there were constant little things in class, micro-aggressions.
My way of dealing with it was,
Everything they said/
Miss?
Everything they said, I would write down/
This man looks like you, miss.
I would write it down and recite back to the student at the end of the class/
Hi Miss/
And say,
Do you realise I've quoted everything you've said to me, and I will be passing this on to your parents?
Whatever

However—and this is interesting—
The parents did not want to hear.
They were so in denial, complete denial. Same with my principal.
In the end, I stopped writing down what they said. I stopped passing it on.
But it felt good to threaten them.
Hi Miss.
Even for a little while.
Do you have a boyfriend Miss?

SFX: PLAYGROUND_BELL_26 SECONDS

Scene 11: Fucking Faggot (Mike)

[MIKE stands centre stage, speaks with composure. RACHEL sits slumped on stool as student, crumpling paper balls and increasingly harasses him from behind, upstage right.]

I've experienced harassment pretty much my whole career.
And it's ranged in terms of intensity.
On some occasions, I'd hear snide comments like, *He bats for the other team,*
Right through to the really, you know, in-your-face, *You fucking faggot,*
That sort of thing.

I wouldn't go shopping after school hours because I would have kids come up to me in the supermarket,

He bats for the other team
Kids who I didn't even teach,
You fucking faggot
And it was really
[beat]
Unnerving. *[smiles]*

That's what made me think I didn't want to teach anymore, after 20—no,
after after 25 years teaching.
That's what led to me having a year off, on stress leave
and also moving back to the city.

See, when I was teaching at a middle school out THERE
In the COUNTRY
I was, sort of,
No. I was outed, by a student.

Because I had a property that neighboured one of my students' property.
Look at him! The fucking faggot.

[angry] And he outed me.
It spread amongst the other boys like wildfire.
Spread it into my private environment, my home life *(beat)*

There were a number of ugly incidents on my property *[smiles]*
Teenage boys on motorbikes
Hooning around outside my home/
Fucking faggot/
Destroying property/
Breaking trees, breaking fences/
You fucking faggot.

The line the school used was, *If it's not happening within the school grounds*
It's not a school matter.
So I contacted the police, but they only suggested I/
Contact the kids' parents/
Which I did.

The parents were livid, fell back on the whole
They're minors, just kids, how dare you.
Like it was **my** fault
How dare/
Like it was up to me/

You/
They blamed me/
Fucking faggot. [beat]
So yeah, I took some time off.

SFX: BELL_SOLO

RACHEL DOES STAND UP GAME #4: SIT DOWN

Using chatterbox, have three audience members pick numbers for three chatterbox games. The answers indicate what the audience will do.

Answer 1: Stand up.

Answer 2: Pick up your paper airplane.

Answer 3: Sit down.

SFX: BELL_SOLO

Scene 12: They Call Me Sir (Dan)

[DAN begins setting up the microphone. RACHEL stands stage right with her back turned, then turns around to play Mr Hall.]

So it's sort of—I don't know.
I basically took up my position here as a lesbian,
as an out lesbian, and they were pretty supportive. I stayed like that for a few years, sort of testing the waters.
But in my fourth year, I went ahead and started to transition. I started taking T over the break,
and I knew it would make some pretty visible, pretty rapid changes.
The school was sort of less supportive then.
There were issues about which toilet I could use, stuff like that./
I came out as male at a staff meeting, and some of the older staff actually stood up and walked out. They were just over it. Queer fatigue.
So yeah./
But I kept going, I felt I had to do this, and that a job shouldn't stop me. The kids were fine.
Sir.
Totally flexible. No judgment, some respectful questions, that's about it.
But the staff? Not so much.//

I had an odd conversation
With one of my Assistant Principals—David, Mr Hall—on the last day of term

148

Just after the assembly – I do the sound system—
[out] Where he noticed that I had some facial hair growing/
What's that—is that? – (flicks face) – is that HAIR?/
[out] /Some facial hair, and was sort of gently mocking/
What's that – you've got something on your face there – (flicks face) – is
that a bit of HAIR?/
And he was asking **how're the kids dealing with it** and, I said –
"Yeah, it's going well, they call me sir for the most part now"/
Oh, they call you sir, that's fantastic.
[beat]
And I was like/
UGH.

[DAN returns to working on mic.]

It's just
It's just this strange idea that if people recognise my male identity, then they
are doing me this big favour, I guess, the school's doing me—
"Oh, they call you sir, that's fantastic."
[beat]

I must admit
I often think about leaving my workplace
And choosing another school.
Part of me doesn't want to until I can fully pass
And be confident in passing, like, close to 100% of the time
Because it would be a lot easier.
A bit of hair? Fancy that.

But if I go to another school
And I'm just a male teacher, what is *that*?
Really, what IS that?
[beat]
It would be a lot easier but. What kind of person would I be?

I'm always going to be the trans teacher *here*,
Which has pros and cons in terms of what
I feel like I could do for the kids.

So if I go to another school
And I'm there as male then—like that's just going to
It would be so bizarre/

To be read as male.

Another **white male teacher in a secondary school!**

So yeah. They call me sir.

Epilogue (Dan and Mr Hall)

Mr Hall: Hello, is this on?

Dan: Yes sir, it's on. Anytime you're ready.

Mr Hall: Alright well done Dan, well done on the hair there. (pokes fun at him again)

Dan: Yes sir, it's hair. That's my hair. My facial hair. My man-hair. And the microphone is on, so anytime you're ready. *David.*

Mr Hall: *[mumbles/speechless]*

Dan: All right. Okay, hello ladies and gentlemen. And congratulations on making it to the last day of our school year. We have had a banner year because of YOU—because of us—our outstanding teachers. We're glad you chose our school. Happy holidays everyone.
Happy Holidays, Sir. *[shakes Mr Hall's hand.]*

Mr Hall: Happy Holidays mate. Hey! –

[MR HALL hands DAN a paper plane and they hold them until bell sounds, then they fly them out into the audience and invite audience to fly theirs onto the stage. The stage is covered in paper airplanes.]

SFX: BELL_PLAYGROUND_SOUNDS 26 SECONDS

[ANNE and RACHEL walk upstage and wait until playground sounds fade.]

PP SLIDE 9: HEAVIER THAN AIR

[bows]

[END OF PLAY]

REVISING/PERFORMING AND...

This chapter detailed our revising process as we moved from the *Out/ In Front* performance to the full production of *Heavier Than Air*. In the revising and performing process, we focused on the feedback we received to the workshop performance in Singapore, considering how words, bodies, things, and spaces come together to create an interactive, moving, and politically powerful performance that honoured the words and lives of the queer teachers that inspired the original research project. As we note in the opening of the chapter, we are now in the process of developing the script for a third production. We've shared this work in process with you to demonstrate how writing for performance is an ongoing and evolving process. When one work is 'finished', another begins. In the concluding chapter, we encourage you to begin (or continue) your own writing for performance projects.

BEGINNINGS, AGAIN

In some ways, the work of writing for performance never ends. The process of writing for the page and the stage means that writers of performance texts see their work in multiple 'versions'—as draft and 'finished' texts, as scripts or blueprints for workshop or rehearsal performances, as works revised for full productions. At each moment, the worlds of words, texts, things, and spaces collide, creating the encounter of performance. Whatever the form your writing takes (or 'genre' it best fits into), words, bodies, things, and spaces ask you to consider the relationships among these elements collectively, as well as how they weave into and through one another (words as things, bodies as spaces, etc.).

And while this book is only one moment in an ongoing conversation about our practices as writers and teachers (of both writing and performance), it is time to turn the page and the stage over to you. As you begin your own writing for performance projects, consider the brief overview of Western performance traditions we shared in Chapter One as a prologue to the elements of writing for performance in the form and performance of Words (Chapter Two), Bodies (Chapter Three), Things (Chapter Four), Spaces (Chapter Five), Rehearsing/Devising (Chapter Six) and Revising/ Performing (Chapter Seven). Check out the twelve exemplars presented throughout the book in more detail. And do the eleven writing exercises presented in Chapters Two through Five as many times as you like. Above all, begin your practice of writing for performance as you would begin a night out at the theatre (or other performance venue, whether that's in the street, at a gallery, in the bathroom on a university campus, or at home in front of your computer screen): with excitement and anticipation about what can happen when word meets page and body meets stage.

As we noted in the first chapter, lists and instructions for beginning our writing often have the opposite effect. They leave us sitting silent and still wondering if we're doing what we think we're doing (writing a play? Creating instructions for a devised work? Creating a verbatim performance or something not-quite so? Writing performance poetry or collage or something not yet named)? They also leave us wondering whether we're doing the writing we're doing—whatever we call it—right and if it is right, whether it's any good. Writing teacher and comic writer Lynda Barry (2008) says two questions began to constrain and haunt her efforts as an artist: "Is this good? Does this suck?" She continues:

> I'm not sure when these two questions became the only two questions I had about my work, or when making pictures and stories turns into something I just called 'my work'—I just know I stopped enjoying it and instead began to dread it… Before the TWO QUESTIONS, pictures and stories happened in a way that didn't involve much thinking. One line led to another until they somehow finished. I never felt like I was trying, and the drawing itself didn't matter too much afterward. (pp. 123, 125)

Barry's narrative calls up both the myriad ways we shut down our work with the voices of criticism—often before we even get started—and the sought-after experience of 'flow' in the writing and creating process (and the 'tricks' we use to get there, several of which are contained in the writing exercises in this book). Barry also reminds us that writing is, above all, an act of performance.

So let's begin, again, remembering what Anne told us in Chapter One (in a slightly different version):

1. There is no one way of doing things.
2. The only thing a writer can control is getting words on the page.
3. Do so in whatever ways work for you.
4. Now it's your turn. Write today's play/one-act/poem/collage/or otherwise-devised performance.

[End of book. For now.]

REFERENCES

A.B. (n.d.). *On my knees.* Unpublished poem.

Ackroyd, J., & O'Toole, J. (2010). *Performing research: Tensions, triumphs and trade-offs of ethnodrama.* London: Institute of Education Press.

Adams, T. E., Holman Jones, S., & Ellis, C. (2015). *Autoethnography.* Oxford: Oxford University Press.

Alexander, B. K. (2005). Performance ethnography. The reinacting and enciting of culture. In N. K. Denzin & Y. S. Lincoln (Eds.), *The Sage handbook of qualitative research* (3rd ed., pp. 411–441). Walnut Creek, CA: Sage.

Amor, A. (2016, February 29). *Performance reflection.* Personal communication.

Amor, A. (n.d.). *Embrace the chaos.* Unpublished poem.

Amor, A. (n.d.). *Four words.* Unpublished poem.

Appaduri, A. (1996). *Moderity at large: Cultural dimensions of globalization* (Public Worlds, Vol. 1). Minneapolis, MN: University of Minnesota Press.

Aristotle. (350 BC). Full text of *The Poetics* (S. H. Butcher, Trans.). *The Internet Classics Archive.* Retrieved from https://www2.cnr.edu/home/bmcmanus/poetics.html

Ash, K., Carlton, S., Evans, G., & Harris, A. (2004). *Surviving Jonah Salt.* Sydney: Playlabs Press.

Auslander, P. (1999/2008). *Liveness: Performance in a mediatized culture.* New York, NY: Routledge.

Auslander, P. (2007). Live from cyberspace, or, I was sitting at my computer this guy appeared he thought I was a bot. In J. G. Reinelt & J. R. Roach (Eds.), *Critical theory and performance* (pp. 522–531). Ann Arbor, MI: University of Michigan Press.

Banes, S. (2010). Olfactory performances. In J. Collins & A. Nisbet (Eds.), *Theatre and performance design: A reader in scenography* (pp. 348–357). Abingdon & New York, NY: Routledge.

Banes, S., & Lepecki, A. (Eds.). (2012/2007). *The senses in performance.* New York, NY: Routledge.

Barry, L. (2008). *What it is.* Montreal: Drawn and Quarterly.

Belluso, J. (n.d.). Retrieved from https://anervoussmile.wordpress.com/john-belluso/

Blau, H. (1990). *The audience.* Baltimore, MD: Johns Hopkins University Press.

Blau, H. (2010). The most concealed object. In J. Collins & A. Nisbet (Eds.), *Theatre and performance design: A reader in scenography* (pp. 49–54). Abingdon & New York, NY: Routledge.

Bottoms, S., & Goulish, M. (Eds). (2007). *Small acts of repair: Performance, ecology, and Goat Island.* London & New York, NY: Routledge.

Boutet, D. (2012). Metaphors of the mind: Art forms as modes of thinking and ways of being. In E. Barrett & B. Bolt (Eds), *Carnal knowledge: Towards a 'new materialism' through the arts* (pp. 29–40). London & New York, NY: IB Tauris & Co Ltd.

Bradby, D. (2001). *Beckett: Waiting for Godot.* Cambridge, UK: Cambridge University Press.

Bradley, M. (Ed). (2015). *Smell and the ancient senses.* New York, NY: Routledge.

Broadhurst, S., & Machon, J. (Eds). (2012). *Identity, performance and technology: Practices of empowerment, embodiment and technicity.* London: Palgrave Macmillan.

Brockelman, T. P. (2001). *The frame and the mirror: On collage and the postmodern.* Evanston, IL: Northwestern University Press.

Brook, P. (1996/1968). *The empty space: A book about the theatre: Deadly, holy, rough, immediate.* New York, NY: Simon and Schuster.

Butler, J. (2015). *Notes toward a performative theory of assembly.* Boston, MA: Harvard University Press.

Cash, L. (2009). *A last, A quartet.* Retrieved from https://vimeo.com/78484997

Chavasta, M. (2005). Remembering praxis: Performance in the digital age. *Text and Performance Quarterly, 25*(2), 156–170.

Chen, W. *They sail across the mirrored sea.* Retrieved from https://www.poets.org/poetsorg/poem/they-sail-across-mirrored-sea

Classen, C., Howes, D., & Synnott, A. (1995). *Aroma: The cultural history of smell.* New York, NY: Routledge.

Collins, J., & Nisbet, A. (Eds.). (2010). *Theatre and performance design: A reader in scenography.* Abingdon & New York, NY: Routledge.

Conquergood, D. (1991). Rethinking ethnography: Towards a critical cultural politics. *Communication Monographs, 58*(2), 179–194.

Conquergood, D. (2002). Performance studies: Interventions and radical research. *The Drama Review, 46*(2), 145–156.

Csikszentmihalyi, M. (2009). *Flow.* New York, NY: HarperCollins.

Cull, L. (2013). *Theatres of immanence: Deleuze and the ethics of performance.* New York, NY: Palgrave MaMillan.

De Benedetto, S. (2011). *The provocation of the senses in contemporary theatre.* New York, NY: Routledge.

Deleuze, G. (1988). *Foucault.* Minneapolis, MN: University of Minnesota Press.

Deleuze, G., & Guattari, F. (1988). *A thousand plateaus: Capitalism and Schizophrenia.* New York, NY: Continuum.

Derrida, J. (1998). *Of grammatology* (G. C. Spivak, Trans.). Baltimore, MD: Johns Hopkins University Press.

Dixon, S. (n.d.). *The IT and audio-visual theatre essay.* Retrieved from http://www.ahds.ac.uk/creating/guides/performing-resources/section3-1.htm

Enright, N. (1999). *Blackrock.* Redfern, New South Wales: Currency Press.

Fensham, R. (2009). *To watch theatre: Essays on genre and corporeality.* New York, NY: Peter Lang.

Forché, C. (1993, March–April). Twentieth century poetry of witness. *American Poetry Review, 22*(2), 17.

Forché, C. (2010). *The angel of history.* New York, NY: HarperCollins.

Fornes, M. I. (1977). *Fefu and her friends.* (publisher not identified).

Gibson, A. K. (2011). *Where do writers write?* Retrieved from http://www.huffingtonpost.com/allison-k-gibson/where-do-writers-write_b_592619.html

Gingrich-Philbrook, C. (2014). A knock at the door: Speculations on theatres and thresholds. *Departures in Critical Qualitative Research, 3*(1), 24–36.

Giovanni, N. *Kidnap poem.* Retrieved from http://www.poemhunter.com/poem/kidnap-poem-3/

Goat Island. (n.d.). *Film.* Retrieved from http://www.goatislandperformance.org/film.htm

Grotowski, J. (2012). *Towards a poor theatre.* New York, NY: Routledge.

Haddad, R. (2016). *Hi, are you single?* Unpublished script.

Hall, S. (Ed.). (1997). *Representation: Cultural representations and signifying practices.* London: Sage Publications.

Hare, D. (2009). *The power of yes: A dramatist seeks to understand the financial crisis.* New York, NY: Faber and Faber.

Harris, A. (2014). *The creative turn: Toward a new aesthetic imaginary.* Rotterdam, The Netherlands: Sense Publishers.

Harris, A., & Farrington, D. (2014). It gets narrower: Creative strategies for re-broadening queer peer education. *Sex Education: Sexuality, Society and Learning, 14*(2), 144–158.

Harris, A., & Gray, E. (Eds.). (2014). *Queer teachers, identity and performativity.* London & New York, NY: Palgrave Macmillan.

Harris, A., & Sinclair, C. (2014). *Critical plays: Embodied research for social change.* Rotterdam, The Netherlands: Sense Publishers.

Hill, L., & Paris, H. (2014). *Performing proximity: Curious intimacies.* New York, NY: Palgrave Macmillan.

Holman Jones, S. (2005). (M)othering loss: Telling adoption stories, telling performativity. *Text and Performance Quarterly, 25*(2), 113–135.

Holman Jones, S. (2009). Crimes against experience. *Cultural Studies<->Critical Methodologies, 9*(5), 608–615.

Holman Jones, S. (2011). Lost and found. *Text and Performance Quarterly, 34*(3), 322–341.

Holman Jones, S. (2014). Always strange: Transforming loss. In J. Wyatt & T. E. Adams (Eds.), *Presence and absence, love and loss: Autoethnographies of parent-child communication* (pp. 13–21). Rotterdam, The Netherlands: Sense Publishers.

Iggulden, A. (2010). 'Silent' speech. In E. Barrett & B. Bolt (Eds.), *Practice as research: Approaches to creative arts enquiry* (pp. 65–80). London & New York, NY: IB Tauris & Co Ltd.

Jameson, F. (1998). *Brecht and method:* London & New York, NY: Verso.

Jenny Holzer. (n.d.). Retrieved from http://www.arthistoryarchive.com/arthistory/contemporary/Jenny-Holzer.html

Jenny Holzer: Multidiscplinary Dweeb. (n.d.). Retrieved from https://www.poets.org/poetsorg/text/jenny-holzer-multidisciplinary-dweeb

Johnson, E. P. (2008). *Sweet tea: Black gay men of the South, an oral history.* Chapel Hill, NC: The University of North Carolina Press.

Jones, A. (1998). *Body art: Performing the subject.* Minneapolis, MN: University of Minneasota Press.

June, T. (2015, June 8). *Fun home* won five Tonys. How did a graphic memoir become a musical? *Slate.* Retrieved from http://www.slate.com/blogs/outward/2013/10/08/fun_home_is_america_ready_for_a_musical_about_a_butch_lesbian.html

Jung, C. (1981). *The archetypes and the collective unconscious* (2nd ed.). New York, NY: Princeton University Press.

Kaufman, M., & Tectonic Theatre. (2001). *The Laramie project.* New York, NY: Vintage Books.

Kilgard, A. (2009). Collage: A paradigm for performance studies. *Liminalities, 5*(3), n.p.

Kilgard, A. (n.d.). *Triskaidekaphobia: 13 consumer tragedies.* Unpublished performance script.

Kurikka, K. (2012). In the name of the author: Toward a materialist understanding of literary authorship. In E. Barrett & B. Bolt (Eds.), *Carnal knowledge: Towards a 'new materialism' through the arts* (pp. 115–126). London & New York, NY: IB Tauris & Co Ltd.

Larbalestier, S. (1990). *The art and craft of collage.* Los Angeles, CA: University of California.

Laurel, B. (2013). *Computers as theatre.* Upper Saddle River, NJ: Addison-Wesley/Pearson.

Leavy, P. (2015). *Method meets art, 2nd edition: Arts-based research practice.* New York, NY: Guilford.

Levan, M. (2005). Elemental spaces, elemental performances. *Performance Research, 10*(4), 120–127.

Lowell, A. *Spring day.* Retrieved from: http://www.poetryfoundation.org/poem/239802

Luton, J. (2015). Pretending to research: Young people at the centre of discovery. In P. O'Connor & M. Anderson (Eds.), *Applied theatre research: Radical departures* (pp. 145–170). New York, NY & London: Bloomsbury.

Madison, D. S. (2012). *Critical ethnography: Method, ethics, and performances.* Walnut Creek, CA: Sage.

Manning, E. (2013). *Always more than one: Individuation's dance.* Durham, NC & London: Duke University Press.

Massumi, B. (2002). *Parables for the virtual: Movement, affect, sensation.* Durham, NC & London: Duke University Press.

McCloud, S. (1994). *Understanding comics: The invisible art.* New York, NY: William Morrow Paperbacks.

McManus, B. F. (1999). Outline of Aristotle's theory of tragedy in the poetics. *CLS 267 Topics Page.* Retrieved from https://www2.cnr.edu/home/bmcmanus/poetics.html

Miller, T. (2002). *Body blows: 6 performances.* Madison, WI: University of Wisconsin Press.

Miller, T. (2006). *1001 beds: Performances, essays and travels.* Madison, WI: University of Wisconsin Press.

Miller, T. (2016). Personal communication.

National Theatre Education. (n.d.). *The hour we knew nothing of each other* by Peter Handke. London: NT Education. Retrieved from http://www.nationaltheatre.org.uk/sites/all/libraries/files/documents/The_Hour_wkpk.pdf

Paris, H. (2002). (Re)Confirming the conventions – An ontology of the olfactory. *Tessera, 32* (Summer 2002), 98–109.

Parks, S. L. (2006). *365 days/365 plays.* New York, NY: Theatre Communications Group.

Pearl, K., & D'Amour. (n.d.). *About.* Retrieved from http://pearldamour.com/?page_id=2

Pearl, K., & D'Amour. (n.d.). *How to build a forest.* Retrieved from http://pearldamour.com/?page_id=33

Perloff, M. (1983). *Collage.* New York, NY: NY Lit Forum.

Perloff, M. (1996). 'Grammar in use': Wittgenstein/Gertrude Stein/Marinetti. *South Central Review, 2/3*(13), 35–62.

Phelan, P. (2003/1993). *Unmarked: The politics of performance.* New York, NY: Routledge.

Poetic Form: Cento. (n.d.). Retrieved from https://www.poets.org/poetsorg/text/poetic-form-cento

Pollock, D. (1998). Performing writing. In P. Phelan & J. Lane (Eds.), *The ends of performance* (pp. 73–103). New York, NY: New York University Press.

Rich, A. (2013). *Diving into the wreck: Poems 1971–1972.* New York, NY: W.W. Norton.

Rickman, A., & Viner, K. (2006). *My name is Rachel Corrie.* New York, NY: Dramatists Play Service.

Roach, R. R. (2007). Mediatized cultures. In J. G. Reinelt & R. R. Roach (Eds.), *Critical theory and performance* (2nd ed., pp. 521–525). Ann Arbor, MI: University of Michigan Press.

Robbins, T. (2001). *Fierce invalids home from hot climates.* New York, NY: Bantam.

Rubin, W. (1968). *Dada, surrealism, and their heritage.* New York, NY: The Museum of Modern Art.

Rudzinzki, C. (2012). *The prayer.* Retrieved from https://www.youtube.com/watch?v=NI155PtD7ZQ

Sachs, N. (1993). But look. In C. Forche (Ed.), *Against forgetting: Twentieth-Century poetry of witness* (p. 363). New York, NY: Norton.

Saldana, J. (Ed.). (2005). *Ethnodrama: An anthology of reality theatre.* Walnut Creek, CA: AltaMira Press.

Saldana, J. (2011). *Ethnotheatre: Research from page to stage.* Walnut Creek, CA: Left Coast Press.

Schechner, R. (2007). Rasaesthetics. In S. Banes & A. Lepecki (Eds.), *The senses in performance* (pp. 10–28). New York, NY: Routledge.

Shepherd-Barr, K. (1999). Mise en scent: The Théâtre d'Art's cantique des cantiques and the use of smell as a theatrical device. *Theatre Research International, 24*(2), 152–159.

Siegel, J. (1995). Jenny Holzer: Language games. *Interview.* Retrieved from https://www.msu.edu/course/ha/452/holzer.html

Sinclair, C., & Harris, A. (2016). Critical plays: An exploration in truth and verisimilitude. In G. Belliveau & G. Lea (Eds.), *Research-based theatre as methodology: An artistic approach to research.* New York, NY: Intellect Books.

Smith, A. D. (2003). *Twilight: Los Angeles 1992.* New York, NY: Dramatists Play Service Inc.

Smith, P. (2015, September 27). Patti Smith: It's not so easy writing about nothing. *The Guardian.* Retrieved from http://www.theguardian.com/music/2015/sep/27/patti-smith-m-train-extract-its-not-so-easy-writing-about-nothing

Smith, S. (1985). Not waving, but drowning. In S. M. Gilbert & S. Gubar (Eds.), *The Norton anthology of literature by women* (p. 1684). New York, NY: Norton.

Spry, T. (2011). *Body, paper, stage: Writing and performing autoethnography.* New York, NY: Routledge.

Stein, G. (1997/1914). *Tender buttons.* New York, NY: Dover.

Stern, N. (2010). *Forms of vitality: Exploring dynamic experience in psychology, the arts, psychotherapy, and development.* Oxford: Oxford University Press.

Stewart, K. (2007). *Ordinary affects.* New York, NY & Durham, NC: Duke University Press.

Taussig, M. (2006). *Walter Benjamin's grave.* Chicago, IL: University of Chicago Press.

Taussig, M. (2011). *I swear I saw this: Drawings in fieldwork notebooks, namely my own.* Chicago, IL: University of Chicago Press.

Tzara, T. (1920). *Dada manifesto on feeble and bitter love.* Retrieved from http://www.391.org/manifestos/1920-dada-manifesto-feeble-love-bitter-love-tristan-tzara.html#.Vs5_ZLTi_5k

Vines, K. (2010). Rhizome/MyZone: A case study in studio-based dance research. In E. Barrett & B. Bolt (Eds.), *Practice as research: Approaches to creative arts enquiry* (pp. 99–112). London & New York, NY: IB Tauris & Co Ltd.

Vroon, P. (1997). *Smell: The secret seducer* (P. Vincent, Trans.). New York, NY: Farrar, Straus and Giroux.

William S. Burroughs Cut-ups. (n.d.). In *Language is a Virus.* Retrieved from http://www.languageisavirus.com/articles/articles.php?subaction= showcomments&id=1099111044&archive=&start_from=&ucat= &#.VtYexrTi_5k

Yates, J. (2010). The briefcase of Walter Benjamin/Benjamin Walter's briefcase: An invent/story. *Rhizomes, 20,* (n.p.). Retrieved from http://rhizomes.net/issue20/ yates/

ABOUT THE AUTHORS

Anne Harris, PhD, is a senior lecturer at Monash University (Melbourne), and researches in the areas of arts, creativity, performance, and diversity. She is a native New Yorker and has worked professionally as a playwright, teaching artist and journalist in the USA and Australia. She has published over 50 articles and 6 books, her latest being *Video As Method* (Oxford University Press, January 2016). She is the book series editor of *Creativity, Education and the Arts* (Palgrave), and a frequent contributor to The Conversation.

Stacy Holman Jones, PhD, is Professor in the Centre for Theatre and Performance at Monash University. Her research and teaching focuses on performance studies theory and practice, gender and critical theory, and critical qualitative methods. She is the author of more than 75 articles, book chapters, reviews, and editorials and the author/editor of 11 books that address performance, culture, identity work and belonging, and social justice and resistance. She is the founding editor of *Departures in Critical Qualitative Research*, a journal dedicated to publishing innovative, experimental, aesthetic, and provocative works on the theories, practices, and possibilities of critical qualitative research.

INDEX

Printed in the United States
by Baker & Taylor Publisher Services